4th Edition
Audit Committee Effectiveness
What Works Best

Prepared by

Principal Authors

Catherine L. Bromilow, CPA

Donald P. Keller, CPA

Project Manager

Garret K. Tripp, CPA, CFE

Sponsored by

IIA–Chicago Chapter

IIA–Philadelphia Chapter

The Institute of Internal Auditors
Research Foundation

ISBN 978-0-89413-708-2
6/11
First Printing

Contents

About the Authors and the Project Team

Principal Authors

Catherine L. Bromilow, CPA, is a partner in PwC's Center for Board Governance. She works with boards of directors and audit committees of major companies and institutions, providing insight on leading practices. She has worked extensively with boards and directors from a number of countries, including the Bahamas, Barbados, Bermuda, Brazil, Canada, Israel, Mexico, the United States, and Venezuela.

For the past 13 years, Catherine has been active in researching and advising on matters relating to board-level governance. She oversees numerous publications for audit committees and boards, including PwC's annual *Current Developments for Directors* and the quarterly periodical *To the Point*. She authored the second and third editions of *Audit Committee Effectiveness — What Works Best*, as well as *Corporate Governance and the Board — What Works Best*. In 2010, for the fourth consecutive year, *NACD Directorship* magazine named her as one of the 100 most influential people in corporate governance in the United States.

Catherine speaks frequently about corporate governance leading practices with boards and at conferences and seminars. She is a Certified Public Accountant (licensed in New Jersey) and a Chartered Accountant (from Canada) and holds a Master of Accounting degree from the University of Waterloo in Canada.

Donald P. Keller, CPA, is a partner in PwC's Center for Board Governance. He focuses on helping corporate directors understand how to address governance challenges and evaluate and benchmark their activities relative to leading practices.

Don has 35 years of experience at PwC, serving as the lead engagement partner for several of the firm's largest multinational clients. His experience includes working with companies on initial public offerings, mergers and acquisitions, and investigations. Don also served as the firm's Global Software Industry Leader, actively addressing software industry issues and business practices and authoring numerous publications and articles. Don brings this insight and experience to help directors address governance challenges and understand the implications of governance developments. He also serves on the faculty of the National Association of Corporate Directors' Director Professionalism Course.

Don is a member of the American Institute of Certified Public Accountants and the Pennsylvania, Texas, New Mexico, and Colorado Societies of CPAs. He has a Bachelor of Business Administration from the University of Notre Dame. He also serves on many not-for-profit boards.

Project Manager

Garret K. Tripp, CPA, CFE, is a senior manager at PwC. During his 11-year career in public accounting, Garret has managed audit engagements for multinational companies and not-for-profit organizations. He has deep experience in the cleantech industry, with a focus on revenue recognition, business acquisitions, and other industry-specific issues. He also has worked with companies in the aerospace and defense industry, specifically focusing on government contracts, government compliance, and related accounting implications. Additionally, Garret has experience with fraud investigations.

Garret is a Certified Public Accountant (licensed in Illinois and Arizona) and a Certified Fraud Examiner, and he holds a Bachelor of Science degree in Accounting from Southern Illinois University at Carbondale.

About PwC and Its Center for Board Governance

PwC firms provide industry-focused assurance, tax, and advisory services to enhance value for their clients. More than 161,000 people in 154 countries in firms across the PwC network share their thinking, experience, and solutions to develop fresh perspectives and practical advice. See www.pwc.com for more information. "PwC" and "PwC US" refer to PricewaterhouseCoopers LLP, a Delaware limited liability partnership, which is a member firm of PricewaterhouseCoopers International Limited, each member firm of which is a separate and independent legal entity.

The mission of PwC's Center for Board Governance is to enhance confidence in corporate governance by providing resources that enable board members to more effectively meet the challenges of their critical role. The Center achieves this objective by sharing leading-edge governance practices, developing insightful and timely thought leadership, and offering forums for directors to discuss contemporary issues.

The Center also engages with boards of directors and audit committees to provide perspectives on significant governance topics and share insights to enhance directors' abilities to comply with evolving regulations and expectations. The Center's collaborations with other governance thought leaders expand the knowledge and value it provides to the director community. Additional information is available at www.pwc.com/us/centerforboardgovernance.

About The IIA Research Foundation

The Institute of Internal Auditors Research Foundation (IIARF) was established by The Institute of Internal Auditors in 1976. Since inception, The IIARF has consistently set the standard for professional achievement in the internal auditing profession. The IIARF's vision is to understand, shape, and advance the global profession of internal auditing by initiating and sponsoring intelligence gathering, innovative research, and knowledge sharing in a timely manner.

As a separate, tax-exempt organization, The IIARF does not receive funding from IIA membership dues but depends on contributions from individuals, organizations, IIA chapters, and institutes to move its programs forward. The IIARF would not be able to function without its valuable volunteers, and thanks the volunteers and contributors who make its successes possible.

Acknowledgments

We appreciate the support of The Institute of Internal Auditors Research Foundation. In particular, we thank Bonnie Ulmer, Vice President, Research, and Nicki Creatore, Research Foundation Operations Manager, for their support. We also thank the volunteer review team, comprised of members of The IIARF's Board of Trustees, Committee of Research and Education Advisors, and The IIA's Chicago and Philadelphia chapters, who offered their time and assistance.

We gratefully acknowledge the many audit committee chairs, internal audit directors, and corporate governance thought leaders who shared their valuable insights and experiences with us. It is their insights that add particular value to this report. Appendix D lists their names and affiliations.

This report also represents the efforts, knowledge, and experience of many PwC professionals from around the world, who generously provided input and advice and assisted with conducting interviews. From Australia, we thank Natalie Abdel-Sayed, Jason Agnoletto, Justin Eve, John Feely, Sian Joubert, Robin Low, Andrew McPherson, Gavin Moss, Andrew Nicolaou, Marisol Reategui, and Mark Ridley. From Brazil, we thank Gustavo Amaral de Lucena and Wilson Marques. From Canada, we thank Brenda Eprile and Mike Harris. From China, we thank Duncan Fitzgerald, Christopher Ho, Cimi Leung, Keith Stephenson, Jasper Xu, Steven Yuan, and Kanus Yue. From France, we thank Jean-Pierre Hottin and Louis-Pierre Schneider. From Germany, we thank Kathrin Kersten, Daniel Korn, Wolfgang Meier, and Maike Mintert. From India, we thank Gaurav Agarwal, Satyavati Berera, Neeraj Gupta, Tapan Ray, and Manpreet Singh Ahuja. From the Middle East, we thank Amit Dutta, Andrew Garrett, Monica Hira, Ahmed Raza Godil, and Madhukar Shenoy. From the Netherlands, we thank Sonja Barendregt-Roojers, Eugenie Krijnsen, Arjan Man, and Haixia Zhu. From Russia, we thank Andrew Cross, Michael Hurle, and Mark Ramsden. From Singapore, we thank Sanjoy Banerjee and Siew Quan Ng. From South Africa, we thank Akhter Moosa, Herman Muller, Paul Prinsloo, Avendth Tilakdari, and Anton van Wyk. From United States, we thank John Barry, Barbara Berlin, Carol Brawley, Brian Brown, Andy Dahle, Elaine Garvey, Sumi Lee, Christopher Michaelson, John Morrow, Ann Pagasky, Charles Reddin, Linda Ross, and Robert Ryan.

How to Use This Book

This publication is intended to be a convenient guide, providing information on topics that are most relevant to the audit committee.

It is a collection of leading practices that supports audit committee performance and effectiveness. It captures insights and points of view from audit committee members, financial reporting experts, governance specialists, and internal audit directors. It also incorporates survey trends, allowing you to understand the financial reporting environment and how audit committees are responding. Just as importantly, it includes lessons learned from the cumulative years of experience of PwC professionals from around the world.

Each chapter is intended to stand alone so you can read and understand the guidance without having to refer to other chapters. Appendix A captures the leading practices from each section and is a useful tool for audit committees when assessing their performance. Additionally, the keyword index allows readers to find discussions about specific topics throughout the book.

This book contains references to rules that are effective at the time of publication. In many cases these are summarized versions of the final rules. Readers should refer to the specific text of the rules and seek appropriate counsel when determining compliance requirements.

Additionally, the practices and procedures described in the book represent suggestions for enhancing the overall performance of the committee and often go beyond applicable rules. A committee should take into consideration its own facts and circumstances when applying these practices.

This book refers to a companion publication, *Board Effectiveness — What Works Best*, 2nd edition. Readers will want to refer to that book for greater insight into the board's role in areas such as risk management, tone at the top, and crisis management.

Executive Summary

The global capital markets rely heavily on the quality of financial statements. The economic crisis that started in 2008 increased the focus on both the role of the audit committee and the information companies disclose. The audit committee's role in ensuring accurate and transparent disclosure is more important today than it has ever been. Clearly, the job is also more difficult and challenging than ever — given increased expectations by shareholders, regulators, and other stakeholders; heightened scrutiny when things go wrong; more responsibility for risk management; and more focus on the need for fraud prevention.

The bottom line is that people expect more from audit committees today, and this publication provides insight into audit committee leading practices that can help committees meet those expectations.

What the chapters cover

1. Financial Reporting and Disclosures

Financial reporting disclosure requirements have been steadily increasing for a number of years, in tandem with the complexity of accounting standards. Regulators and financial statement users continue to press companies for more information and to get that information sooner. This environment makes the audit committee's responsibility to oversee the company's financial reporting more difficult. The committee must be aware of the financial reporting risks to focus its attention appropriately. And it cannot lose sight of the need to maintain its skepticism. This chapter highlights ways the committee can best understand and monitor the company's financial reporting.

2. Risk Management and the System of Internal Control

Given how many risks — known and unknown — a company faces, it's a challenge for a board or audit committee to get comfortable that the company is addressing risk appropriately. One of the difficulties facing the audit committee is clearly defining its risk responsibility relative to that of the entire board. While the company's system of internal control is designed to help mitigate risk, the audit committee focuses particularly on controls relating to financial reporting, fraud, and compliance. This chapter helps the committee to better understand the risks that most likely fall within its scope and how to monitor whether the company is addressing those risks appropriately.

3. Culture and Compliance — The Soul of Corporate Accountability

The company's culture and code of conduct are critical factors in creating an environment that encourages compliance with laws and regulations. The audit committee must recognize how critical the right tone at the top of the company is and ensure what it's hearing in the boardroom is what employees are hearing throughout the company. This chapter provides insights that help the committee understand what elements compliance programs should have to promote proper conduct and behavior throughout the company.

4. Oversight of Management and Internal Audit

The audit committee needs to oversee management while taking care not to step into management's role. Establishing an effective relationship with management is essential — it allows the committee to effectively monitor the company's financial reporting practices and evaluate management's competence. Similarly, the committee relies heavily on internal audit to provide an objective view on how the company is handling a number of key risks, including those relating to financial reporting and compliance. This chapter discusses how the committee builds effective relationships with both management and internal audit.

5. Relationship with External Auditors

The audit committee has to select the right external auditors to conduct a quality audit. As part of executing their audit plan, the external auditors provide the audit committee with assurance regarding the company's financial reporting. Additionally, external auditors are in a unique position to provide unfiltered and unbiased feedback to the committee about management and the company's processes. This chapter guides the committee through the ways to evaluate and appoint auditors and to develop and maximize the value of external audit relationships.

6. What to Do When Things Go Wrong — Financial Statement Errors and Fraud Investigations

At times, breakdowns in financial reporting processes lead to potential errors in previously issued financial statements. Management and the audit committee have to assess whether an error is material and, if it is, take steps to resolve the situation. The situation can become more complex if the error results from fraud. The committee also might have to become involved when allegations arise of bribery or other forms of fraud. In such cases, the committee may have to oversee an investigation. This chapter discusses factors for the committee when it must consider a possible restatement or oversee an investigation.

7. Committee Composition

Composition and leadership are critical in supporting the audit committee's ability to carry out its responsibilities effectively. The committee needs the right combination of skills and experience. It also needs a chair with the knowledge and commitment to drive the committee's work. This chapter discusses considerations for selecting committee members and the chair and for determining how large the committee should be.

8. Meetings

To ensure committee meetings run well, the committee needs to have the right agenda and receive the right materials beforehand. The attendees, and how they interact with committee members, also influence the success of meetings. Given how many responsibilities the committee has, it needs to ensure it is meeting often enough and at the right points during the year. This chapter describes ways the committee can create an effective meeting environment, allowing the members to engage in meaningful discussion and make the most of private sessions.

9. Supporting Committee Effectiveness — Charter, Evaluations, Resources, and Training

The charter documents the audit committee's purpose, roles, and responsibilities. It helps distinguish the committee's responsibilities from those of the full board of directors. An audit committee that periodically evaluates its performance will be able to identify ways to improve its effectiveness. Orientation training for new members and ongoing development for all members are essential, particularly given the velocity of changes to financial reporting and governance standards. This chapter discusses considerations for the committee's charter, methods the committee can use to assess its performance, and ways to meet its training objectives.

1

Financial Reporting and Disclosures

Although an audit committee may take on many additional responsibilities — such as those discussed in following chapters — its central responsibility is to oversee the integrity of the company's financial statements and related disclosures. Audit committees receive a great deal of financial information, and it can be challenging to understand the complex issues and determine how best to oversee financial reporting. The financial statements are the key way a company communicates its results to shareholders.

Chapter 1 supports the committee's understanding and monitoring of the financial reporting function. This chapter also stresses the importance of the committee's focus on areas that are new or different from prior reports, including any changes stemming from economic conditions, business strategy, or new accounting policies. Of course it's essential that committees bring the appropriate level of skepticism to this review, by asking probing questions and having frank discussions with management and the auditors.

The good news is that generally, boards of directors have confidence in their audit committees' ability to monitor accurate financial reporting. In the PwC *2010 Annual Corporate Directors Survey,* 97% of directors rate their audit committee as "very effective" or "effective."

This chapter addresses the following elements supporting audit committees' effectiveness in overseeing companies' financial reporting processes:

1. Understanding the business

2. Staying focused — complex, difficult, and riskier areas

3. Materiality

4. Accounting policies

5. Accounting estimates

6. Significant changes during the reporting period

7. Related party transactions

8. Special items, including non-GAAP disclosures

9. Interim financial statements

10. Management disclosure committees

11. Narrative reporting and transparency

12. Earnings guidance

13. Correspondence with securities regulators

14. Timing issues

1 | *Understanding the business*

Audit committee members need a robust knowledge of the company, its operations, and its industry to assess financial reports effectively. Exhibit 1.1 suggests ways to build this knowledge.

Exhibit 1.1	How to enhance understanding of the business

- Review the "business" discussion included in past annual reports
- Visit company operations, plants, and facilities
- Meet with marketing and sales management to gain insight into products and markets
- Understand the sales distribution channel and who major customers are
- Understand the supply chain and who the major suppliers are
- Meet with business unit leaders to grasp operational details
- Meet with finance management, internal audit, and the external auditors
- Review analysts' reports about the company, its competitors, and the industry
- Listen to management's calls with analysts and responses to analysts' questions
- Review competitor financial statements and nonfinancial information

- Leverage any electronic clipping service that management uses, including relevant articles from industry-focused publications
- Inquire of management what Internet information is being posted about the company (e.g., on message boards or blogs)
- Understand major business transactions and changes during the period
- Understand the company's regulators, the impact on the company of political or public pressure the regulators may be under, the approach taken to regulating the company and the industry, and significant regulatory issues
- Meet with finance, taxation, and treasury personnel to understand capital structure, tax structure, and hedging activities
- Review reports by rating agencies for the company's debt

Audit committee members likely will gain some of this knowledge as part of their role on the board of directors.

Some audit committees strengthen their understanding of the business by holding one or two meetings each year at an operating site. Others have business unit heads periodically attend a meeting to provide insights into their area of the company.

Interview insights
Listening to replays of analysts' calls is a great way to determine how the outside world views our company.
– AC Chair

Interview insights
Having a profound knowledge of the business is a key element of ensuring our financial reports properly portray the company.
– AC Chair

Interview insights
Our audit committee often meets at different operating plants. Getting away from our corporate offices provides more insight to the committee members.
– IA Director

2 | *Staying focused — complex, difficult, and riskier areas*

A company generally has certain business units or areas that are much more complex and challenging to understand than routine areas such as payroll. Management should highlight such complex or risky areas for the audit committee. Those areas may include hedging operations or off-balance sheet structures. By focusing on such areas, audit committees can review financial statements and related information more efficiently and effectively, especially given their limited meeting time.

Effective audit committees request targeted information relating to complex areas. Exhibit 1.2 shows one approach covering a revenue cycle for a particular product line.

Exhibit 1.2	Assessing revenue recognition and related accounts receivable		
	Prior Year End Balance	Current Year End Balance	Change
Revenue	$6 million	$6.6 million	10%
Accounts Receivable	$.750 million	$1 million	33%

Current business issues: Customers can return new products, such as version 6.0 of our cell phone, after a 30-day trial period if they believe they are not performing to specifications. This makes estimating reserves for returns highly judgmental, and we do not have significant experience with this newer technology. Our return rate for the new version increased during the last quarter because of customer dissatisfaction. Also, strengthening of the U.S. dollar has made our product more expensive in Asian markets than we had expected. Competitors have introduced competing products in Asian markets, which could require us to reconsider our current pricing structure.

Critical aspects: Analysts and investors focus on our revenue growth rate, which significantly impacts our stock price. Increases in days sales outstanding and accounts receivable balances can raise questions as to whether the customer has actually accepted the goods and whether some sales could be reversed in future periods.

Accounting policies: Revenue is recorded when title and risk of loss transfer to the customer, collectibility is assured, and price is determinable. A high degree of judgment is involved in estimating the reserve for returns.

Other relevant information: Customers gained (to date) from new version 6.0 — 24,000; market share increased from 9% to 10.2% since product release; reserve for returns recorded at 3% of sales versus 2.8% in prior quarter.

3 | *Materiality*

Materiality is central to financial reporting. Management uses materiality when evaluating whether to disclose an item, assessing whether to make a proposed adjustment, determining the magnitude of an internal control deficiency, and deciding whether to restate previously issued financial statements. The audit committee should understand how management and external auditors evaluate materiality and have its own views on the level of materiality.

Establishing materiality can be quite complex. For example, some point to a "rule of thumb" quantitative threshold (e.g., 5% of net income or net loss) to establish materiality. It is not unusual to use different quantitative thresholds for assessing the materiality in interim financial results versus annual results.

While a quantitative threshold is useful for preliminarily assessing whether an item is likely to be material, securities regulators caution that there is no real basis for any percentage or numerical thresholds. Materiality is more than just a quantitative concept, and significant judgment is involved in evaluating it qualitatively. In essence, an error is material if it is large enough that it could change or influence a user's judgment. And so management and the auditors need to assess all relevant quantitative and qualitative facts and circumstances before being satisfied that an item is in fact immaterial.

U.S. Securities and Exchange Commission (SEC) guidance directs companies to consider that a quantitatively small error may be material if it:

- *Masks changes* in earnings or other trends, especially trends in profitability and earnings per share

- *Hides a failure* to meet analysts' consensus expectations for the company

- *Changes a loss* into income, or vice versa

- *Helps conceal an unlawful transaction* or involves improper acts by senior management

- *Affects the company's compliance* with loan covenants, other contractual agreements, or regulatory requirements

- *Concerns a segment* or part of the business that has been identified as playing a significant role in the company's operations or profitability

- *Increases management's compensation* — for example, by satisfying threshold requirements for bonus awards or other forms of incentive compensation

Materiality is more than just a quantitative concept — significant judgment is involved.

Management also uses materiality to evaluate the effect of any internal control deficiencies. U.S. companies use the following categories when assessing deficiencies in internal control over financial reporting:

- *Material weakness:* A deficiency or combination of deficiencies, such that there is a reasonable possibility that a material misstatement of the company's annual or interim financial statements will not be prevented or detected on a timely basis.

- *Significant deficiency:* A deficiency or a combination of deficiencies that is less severe than a material weakness, yet important enough to merit attention by the audit committee.

Likewise, the external auditors also establish materiality guidelines, as described in Exhibit 1.3. Audit committees can find it useful to discuss materiality thresholds with the external auditors, to gain additional insight into how the auditors assess financial reporting issues and to evaluate the degree to which the auditors' view of materiality differs from management's view.

Exhibit 1.3	External auditors' materiality judgments

Audit planning materiality: Used to determine which classes of transactions, account balances, and disclosures should be subject to audit testing.

Audit adjustment threshold: Used to determine whether the company is required to record an identified audit adjustment to receive an unqualified audit opinion. Also used to consider whether to include adjustments in the summary of uncorrected misstatements, which is communicated to the audit committee. Many believe that all identified audit adjustments that are communicated to the audit committee should be reflected in the financial statements.

Assessments of control deficiencies: Used to determine whether a control deficiency is a material weakness, a significant deficiency, or a deficiency when auditors issue an opinion on the effectiveness of a company's internal control over financial reporting.

Materiality levels are important because they drive decisions on the need for a restatement. As Chapter 6 discusses, those are always difficult judgments for a number of reasons. Plus, following the economic crisis, more companies adopted policies to recoup or "claw back" compensation following a restatement. Indeed, rules expected in 2011 will require U.S. public companies to have such clawback policies to recover excess incentive compensation paid to executives. Audit committees should recognize that the presence of such policies could potentially influence how management sets materiality and considers the need for a restatement.

Astute audit committees recognize that materiality assessments are an ongoing process. For example, at the beginning of a period, management may establish materiality assuming the company's projected income or loss will be at a certain level. If those projected results are not met, management and the external auditors may need to adjust their thresholds of materiality from those originally established.

4 | *Accounting policies*

It is critical that audit committees understand the significant accounting policies the company uses and whether they are reasonable and appropriate. Because of the volume and complexity of accounting standards, leading audit committees are devoting time at meetings to ensure they understand existing accounting policies. The most significant accounting policies are typically included in the first or second footnote to the financial statements. As important as the accounting policies themselves is the manner in which management interprets and applies them to a particular class of transactions. (Indeed, external auditors are required by auditing standards to provide specific information to the audit committee on the company's accounting policies, along with other required communications as described in Appendix C.)

The audit committee can gain valuable information from asking both the investor relations officer and management if criticisms of the company's accounting policies have surfaced — whether from the public, short sellers, or anonymously through the whistleblower program. If so, the committee should understand the nature of the critiques and discuss them with management, legal counsel, and the external auditors.

Companies and audit committees ignore such criticism at their peril. In many well-publicized instances the criticism was valid, and companies ultimately had to restate their financial statements. They then had to cope with adverse investor and market reaction, loss of reputation, and lawsuits (as discussed in Chapter 6).

When considering existing accounting policies, audit committees should ask such questions as:

- Is management interpreting the policies in an overly conservative or aggressive manner?
- Do the accounting policies appear appropriate based on the substance of the transactions?
- What methods do major competitors use?

- Are there any alternative acceptable accounting policies?
- If alternatives exist, do the external auditors agree the existing accounting policies are the "preferable" ones?

One effective way audit committees ensure they understand critical accounting policies is to set aside committee meeting time to focus on one specific accounting policy. This might entail a specific training session on revenue recognition, for example.

Although it's done infrequently, management may voluntarily change accounting policies if it believes a different policy more appropriately reflects the economics of a transaction. This could be due to a switch in how the company conducts its business, to a particular matter becoming more significant, or to changed facts and circumstances. For U.S. public companies, external auditors have to issue a letter to the SEC indicating whether a change to an alternative accounting principle is, in their judgment, preferable in the circumstances. In many other countries, companies are required to demonstrate that a new accounting policy is more "relevant and reliable."

Interview insights
When new accounting developments are announced, the audit committee discusses with the CFO and external auditors how it will impact the results and financial disclosures. The CFO also indicates whether he has adequate resources to handle the new requirements.
– AC Chair

Interview insights
Changes in accounting standards can be significant, and the audit committee relies on the finance department and the external auditors to keep the committee up to date. Being aware of these changes in advance allows us to ensure all parties are properly aligned.
– AC Chair

Such requirements provide audit committees with additional assurance that the change is appropriate.

If management is proposing a discretionary change in accounting policies, audit committees might consider questions such as:

- Why is the change being proposed?
- What is "preferable" about the change?
- If it is a change to adopt a "preferable" method, why was it not used in previous years?
- Have regulators ever questioned the existing policy?
- What will the effect on income be for the current and future periods?

- What effect will the change have on the company's loan covenants?
- What effect will the change have on executive compensation or bonus plans?
- Will regulators, shareholders, or analysts object to the change?
- What are the consequences of not implementing the change?

Sometimes it can be challenging to understand whether an accounting change relates to a change in policy or simply a change in estimate, particularly in different countries. For example, in the United States, selecting a different depreciation method would be a change in policy, whereas changing depreciable lives would constitute a change in estimate. But under International Financial Reporting Standards, both are considered changes in estimates.

Of course, the other reason companies change their accounting policies is that they are required to, stemming from a change in accounting standards or securities regulatory rules. Ideally, the committee should be briefed long before a new accounting standard will affect the company's financial statements. Indeed, companies often have to disclose the potential impact of adopting new accounting standards.

Accordingly, the audit committee should discuss with management and the external auditors:

- New standards affecting the company in the current year
- New standards that will affect the company in a future year

- The financial statement implications of new standards, as well as what the company intends to disclose
- Standards under development and how, when adopted, they might affect the company's financial statements

5 | Accounting estimates

Accounting estimates represent higher financial reporting risk and require significant judgment by management. Accordingly, the audit committee should understand which areas involve estimates, given their effect on reported results. Management commonly makes estimations for:

- Uncollectible accounts receivable
- Slow-moving or obsolete inventory
- Asset impairment
- Pension and other postemployment benefit obligations
- Income tax exposures

- Derivatives valuations
- Warranty liabilities
- Litigation reserves
- Environmental liabilities
- Stock option expenses
- Restructuring costs

For many of these estimates, management must predict the effects of events that might not occur until future reporting periods. Management typically determines accounting estimates based on a range of possible acceptable balances in the spectrum from aggressive to conservative. The degree of conservatism may significantly affect the amount management records.

Exhibit 1.4	Reasonable ranges for estimates						
(In millions)	Beginning of Period			End of Period			Impact on Pre-tax Earnings
	Reasonable Range			Reasonable Range			
Account	Conservative	Aggressive	Recorded Balance	Conservative	Aggressive	Recorded Balance	
Environmental Liability	$1.4	$1.2	$1.4	$1.2	$1.0	$1.0	$.4
Litigation Reserves	$2.8	$2.5	$2.8	$2.8	$2.3	$2.3	$.5
Total							$.9

As Exhibit 1.4 shows, if management had used the conservative estimate at the end of the period as it did at the beginning, the current period pre-tax earnings would have increased by only $200,000. Audit committees should understand the rationale if management changes the degree of conservatism used in determining estimates. As discussed in Appendix C, a proposed (at the time of this publication) U.S. auditing standard would require external auditors to communicate specific information to the audit committee when critical accounting estimates involve a range of possible outcomes, including how the recorded estimates relate to the range and how various selections within the range would affect the company's financial statements.

While many companies have well-established methods for handling relatively routine estimates, other estimates can prove more difficult. Management may need to use significant judgment to determine the appropriate amount to record. While recognizing that estimates are highly subjective, some committees still do not fully appreciate the extent to which management could improperly "manage" earnings by manipulating assumptions and estimates, and so they fail to give this area enough attention. As a result, audit committees should devote time to focus on management's process for developing estimates. For example, calculating the liability for pension benefits involves numerous assumptions such as return on assets, discount rate, salary increases, etc. Minor changes in any of these assumptions could have a material impact on the amount of the liability or expense. Accordingly, the audit committee should understand how management determines such estimates and how the assumptions used compare to previous periods.

Audit committees can embrace leading practices for overseeing accounting estimates by:

- Understanding which financial statement accounts contain important estimates. One way to check completeness is to review nonstandard representations included in the management representation letter that is provided to the external auditors, as those often indicate highly judgmental areas.

- Discussing with management the quality of processes and systems and the reliability of data underlying estimates

- Considering how estimates historically matched up against actual results

- Understanding key business assumptions and dependencies supporting estimates and whether those assumptions changed or should have changed

- Understanding the extent to which management uses models in developing estimates and how it ensures those models are valid (perhaps through engaging third parties to test complex models for pension or derivatives valuations)

- Understanding the likelihood that underlying events will occur

- Understanding why management did, or chose not to, record a particular estimate and whether balances continue to be appropriate

- Understanding the reasons underlying the timing and amounts of accruals, such as restructuring provisions and asset write-downs

- Understanding how much a minor change in an assumption would change the recorded amount

- Engaging auditors or other third-party experts to test and validate models that are particularly significant and complex

By considering such factors and applying its knowledge of the company's business performance, the committee can form an opinion about whether key accounting estimates are reasonable.

> *While recognizing that estimates are highly subjective, some committees still do not fully appreciate the extent to which management could improperly "manage" earnings by manipulating assumptions and estimates.*

6 | *Significant changes during the reporting period*

Audit committees should review significant period-to-period changes in the financial statements. Management will need to provide substantive explanations for such changes and for major variations between actual results and budgets or forecasts.

Astute audit committees also inquire whether there are significant increases in volume (particularly revenue) directly before the period-end close. They also look for significant changes between the early part of the reporting period versus the last few weeks, unless this type of fluctuation is inherent in the business. Additionally, they ask management to address why significant variances did not occur if the committee has operational or other information that indicates there should be changes. And astute committee members challenge management when earnings information provided earlier in the period suggested targets would not be met, and yet at period end they were.

Importantly, if management recorded any unusual or nonrecurring transactions, committees should understand the nature of such transactions, their economic substance, and their effect on the financial statements and also should consider whether the accounting and disclosures are appropriate. Management's explanations need to be reasonable and consistent with the committee's understanding of the company. The audit committee should also obtain explanations for any significant changes in estimates that involve a high degree of estimation and judgment. Exhibit 1.5 provides an example of how management might provide such information to the committee.

Exhibit 1.5	Sales returns fluctuation analysis		
(In millions)	Balance End of Period	Balance Beginning of Period	Change
Sales Returns Reserve	€11.1	€10.5	€.6

Management analysis: The sales returns reserve balance increased by €600,000 during the period, which reduced pretax earnings by the same amount. Of the increased balance, 1) approximately €250,000 is due to a deterioration of our aged accounts receivable, using a consistent methodology to perform the calculation; 2) approximately €200,000 relates to a distributor that is experiencing financial difficulty and may not be able to pay amounts owed; 3) approximately €125,000 relates to increased sales volumes over the previous period, using a consistent methodology to calculate the necessary reserve; and 4) approximately €25,000 relates to miscellaneous items.

7 | *Related party transactions*

A particularly sensitive area of financial reporting involves related party transactions. Why? Because such transactions cannot be presumed to have been carried out on an arm's-length basis. That's one reason proxy advisory firms and shareholders scrutinize related party transactions, particularly those involving directors and executives. A challenge for audit committees is that they may be unaware the company has entered into transactions involving related parties, and so don't have a good basis for determining whether the disclosures are adequate.

Related parties typically include:

- Affiliates of the company, which would include board directors

- Investees of the company where the company has significant influence over the operations

- The company's principal owners and management and their immediate family members

- Other parties with whom the company deals, if either one can significantly influence the operations of the other

Related party transactions can take many forms. For example, a director may be an executive at one of the company's significant customers or suppliers. Or, the company may have transactions with a significant shareholder. Sometimes, these types of transactions can include potential conflicts of interest or even involve nonmonetary consideration.

Companies have to disclose material related party transactions in financial statements — other than certain transactions such as compensation arrangements entered into in the ordinary course of business. These disclosures typically provide the nature of the relationships involved, a description of the transactions during the period, the dollar amounts involved, amounts due from or to the related party, and any other information users need to understand the effects of the transactions on the financial statements.

Given the sensitivity of such disclosures, astute audit committees check that management has an adequate process to identify related parties, capture transactions with them, and provide sufficient disclosures. Committees recognize it's important these disclosures be complete and provide all the necessary information, including possibly the reason for the relationship, so financial statement users can understand the transactions.

8 | Special items, including non-GAAP disclosures

Companies sometimes separate out particular transactions or events when reporting to shareholders. Management might view these items as nonrecurring, infrequent, or unusual in nature and believe that highlighting them is warranted, given their anomalous effect on current earnings. Analysts and investors typically follow suit, and exclude the impact of those transactions when evaluating company performance or forecasting earnings. And analysts' views can have a significant effect on a company's share price. Some observers and securities regulators are concerned such disclosures might mask the company's true earnings and that management's approach may be inconsistent from one period to another — that management highlights only the good items and backs out the bad items. So it's important for audit committees to understand the company's proposed disclosures of such items and the effect of such disclosures.

Judgment is needed to determine what constitutes a "special" item that should be separately communicated to financial statement users. Generally accepted accounting principles don't address this concept, and so such disclosures are often outside the confines of established accounting standards.

Effective audit committees discuss unusual items with management and the external auditors. Exhibit 1.6 below provides an example of how management could summarize such information for the audit committee to enhance its understanding of the unusual items that occurred and to facilitate the discussion of what special items the company plans to call out separately in the earnings release.

Interview insights
Our audit committee spends significant time on transactions and results which appear out of the ordinary and seeks explanations on these from management and the auditors.

– AC Chair

Exhibit 1.6	Unusual items recorded during the period		
(In millions)	Pre-tax Effect	After-tax Effect	Impact on Earnings per Share
Plant Closure in Florida Due to Hurricane	$5.0	$3.2	$.02
Workers' Strike in France	$8.0	$4.8	$.03
Settlement of Lawsuit	($10.0)	($6.5)	($.04)
Power Outage in Mexico	$1.0	$.7	$.01
Total Impact to Period	$4.0	$2.2	$.02

In the United States, the term "non-GAAP" disclosures refers to certain performance measures (e.g., earnings before interest, taxes, depreciation, and amortization — EBITDA) as well as the reporting of earnings or earnings per share that excludes the impact of unusual items. While the SEC allows these disclosures, it calls for management to acknowledge that the data is not in accordance with generally accepted accounting principles and to provide the reason management believes such information is useful. Companies are also required to present the most comparable GAAP measures with equal or greater prominence, along with a reconciliation between the two measures.

Audit committees will want to:

- Be aware of the impact of unusual items recorded in the period

- Understand whether management plans to separate the impact of these issues from reported earnings

- Understand whether management is consistent in the way it treats special items across periods

- Ask whether the company is consistent in all of its communications — in websites, earnings releases, investor calls, and analyst reports — understanding that regulators also are scrutinizing these communications for consistency

- Understand management's rationale for providing any alternative measures of performance

The bottom line is the committee should be comfortable that the disclosures of special items and non-GAAP measures are consistently applied across reporting periods and different types of communications and that they are not misleading.

9 | *Interim financial statements*

Complete and consistent interim reports are just as important as annual financial statements to lenders, investors, and analysts. Typically, companies provide limited interim financial information — first in a press release and subsequently, in a more comprehensive manner, in a regulatory filing. Audit committees should take an active role overseeing interim financial statements and related disclosures.

Astute committees perform their review before the company issues the interim financial information, rather than after the fact. The Smith Guidance in the U.K. Combined Code requires board-level oversight of interim reports — and this usually falls to the audit committee. The New York Stock Exchange (NYSE) rules require audit committees to review quarterly financial statements. The Securities and Exchange Board of India places similar requirements on audit committees.

During its review of interim results, an audit committee should ask management about significant judgments and issues faced in the period-end closing and whether the interim statements were prepared on a basis consistent with the annual financial statements. Many questions posed during the annual review — how results compare with budget, whether accounting policies are consistently applied, if there are significant changes in trends or significant transactions, how unusual events are reflected, the overall quality of earnings, and the adequacy of proposed disclosures — apply to interim reports as well.

The audit committee also should discuss the results of any external auditor review of an interim report. As is the case with annual financial statements, external auditors are required to communicate specific matters to the committee (see Appendix C) — including the selection of new or changes to significant accounting policies, adjustments identified during the review, material accounting or disclosure errors identified, disagreements with management, and material changes in internal control. Such communications should take place before the interim report is filed with securities regulators; in many cases, audit committees hold these discussions before the press release is issued. The audit committee often discusses interim results with management and the external auditors via a conference call, rather than meeting in person.

10 | *Management disclosure committees*

Management needs to ensure the financial information reported to shareholders includes all the transactions and disclosures it should and is recorded, processed, and summarized accurately.

Indeed, CEOs and CFOs of U.S. public companies must certify to the material fairness of the financial statements and the effectiveness of related financial reporting controls and procedures. U.S. companies often establish management-level disclosure committees to support these certifications. Such committees typically comprise management from operations as well as finance and legal. The disclosure committee helps ensure the completeness of information reported and discusses other reporting issues and developments arising during each period. Many companies require additional certifications from managers at many levels companywide, and so disclosure committees also address any exceptions identified or issues raised in this broader certification process. In other countries, companies also have these disclosure reviews, which typically involve the attendees listed above, although they are not performed by a formally designated "disclosure committee."

The Conference Board's *2010 U.S. Directors' Compensation and Board Practices Report* indicates that more than 70% of companies have a management-level disclosure committee.

Audit committees should understand what processes management uses to ensure its financial reports capture all relevant data. In some companies, the disclosure committee periodically reports on its activities to the audit committee. Such information provides additional assurance that financial statements are accurate and complete.

11 | *Narrative reporting and transparency*

Public companies in a number of countries must provide additional disclosure of risks and results. In the United Kingdom, companies provide operating and financial reviews. In a number of countries including the United States and India, these disclosures take the form of management's discussion and analysis (MD&A.) Indeed, the NYSE rules require the audit committee to review the company's MD&A disclosures. External auditors are also required to communicate whether the narrative reporting accompanying financial statements is consistent with the financial statements and the auditors' knowledge of the company's results. Whatever form the reporting takes, the audit committee should review it before release and consider whether it is consistent with the financial statements and the committee's understanding of what has happened at the company.

Although securities regulators encourage meaningful and robust disclosure, companies have some choice in what they disclose. Companies that have committed to transparency disclose more information — for example, their competitive market environment, company strategy, business activities, targets and results for key performance measures, and detailed segment information. And once they start, they provide this information consistently, even when it may reflect unfavorably on the company.

Transparent communications successfully convey to investors and other stakeholders information they need to understand and value the business and to make decisions, such as whether to join the company as an employee or do business with it as a customer or supplier. For example, manufacturers may release information about plant capacity; software companies may comment on license sales; publishers, about circulation numbers; and pharmaceutical companies, about results of testing and research studies.

Assessing whether the information in narrative reports is accurate is really only part of a committee's role. Audit committees also should consider whether the reporting is complete. Is the company disclosing what it should? Is it providing the full story? Do these results really reflect the ongoing, sustainable operations of the business? Does some of the information distort the real results?

What happens when the committee identifies something management has proposed to omit? It needs to challenge management as to the reasons why the item should or should not be disclosed. If the discussion convinces the committee, then it will accept management's viewpoint. However, if the committee isn't convinced — say, management opposes disclosing an item because it might benefit competitors, yet the committee believes financial statement users should have this information — it should demand disclosure. Not disclosing information because the company could be embarrassed is not a supportable rationale.

Securities regulators also ask companies to explain why they didn't provide earlier warnings of potentially significant adverse events. Financial statement users want to understand the degree of risk associated with (and possible changes to) recorded estimates, liquidity, ratios, contingency reserves, and other potential occurrences, if management has identified the matters when the financial statements are released. For example, if it is reasonably likely that a major customer could declare bankruptcy and be unable to pay the company, shareholders would want to understand this uncertainty.

Similarly, if management is aware that significant warranty costs could be incurred because of a potential product recall that is "reasonably likely" to occur in a future period, there may be an expectation that the company would disclose this uncertainty and the impact on the warranty accrual. Indeed, when an adverse event occurs, regulators and others — such as plaintiffs' lawyers — will, using hindsight, try to determine whether the company should have known it was possible and disclosed it.

When reviewing narrative reporting and other such disclosures, audit committees should consider whether the reporting:

- Provides real analysis, enabling investors to see the company through the eyes of management and to understand key financial and nonfinancial indicators management uses

- Enhances the overall financial disclosure and provides a context for analyzing the company's financial condition

- Provides information about the quality and potential variability of the company's earnings and cash flows, so investors can determine the likelihood that past performance is indicative of future performance

- Is clear, candid, and written in plain language for understandability

- Gives greatest prominence to the most important information

- Discusses known material events, trends, and uncertainties that would indicate the company's past performance is not necessarily indicative of future results — for example, matters that may require adjustment in future periods

- Describes the company's ability to meet both short- and long-term cash requirements

- Is consistent and comparable from period to period and compared with past results, industry norms, and management expectations

- Provides additional insight, instead of simply repeating information from the financial statement footnotes

- Complies with the spirit of relevant professional and regulatory disclosure requirements, reporting not just the form, but also the substance of transactions

- Provides forward-looking perspective about expected trends of the business, market, industry, competitive factors, etc.

One philosophy regarding disclosure and transparency is to view information required for regulatory or statutory reporting as the minimum the company should disclose. Audit committee members should then consider what additional information would be important to investors and other users of financial reports.

12 | *Earnings guidance*

In addition to issuing financial statements, companies frequently provide earnings guidance and other forward-looking information. Investors, analysts, lenders, and securities regulators closely monitor this information. Some observers are concerned that issuing earnings or other performance guidance places undue pressure on management, and may in turn affect management's financial reporting judgments and estimates.

Audit committees should ideally be part of the review process for such financial information. Indeed, the NYSE rules require audit committees to discuss earnings press releases, as well as the financial information and earnings guidance provided to analysts and rating agencies. The rules allow audit committees to have a general discussion (i.e., discuss the types of information to be disclosed or the types of presentations to be made) and do not require that the discussion be held in advance of each release. Canadian Securities Administrators rules also recommend that audit committees review earnings press releases. The audit committee's review of earnings press releases also is general practice in other countries, including Australia.

Many companies provide earnings guidance. The Conference Board's *2010 U.S. Directors' Compensation and Board Practices Report* shows 40% of responding companies provide quarterly earnings guidance, and most expect to continue providing it.

> *Interview insights*
> The audit committee needs to understand consensus guidance since guidance can drive behavior in nonconstructive ways.
> – AC Chair

In reviewing forward-looking guidance, astute audit committees:

- Understand what guidance the company provides (e.g., revenue growth, earnings per share, cash flows)

- Understand how management accumulates the underlying information

- Understand key business assumptions and dependencies used to develop the guidance

- Discuss the likelihood of business assumptions occurring

- Consider management's history in meeting targets and whether the company is in a credible position to provide forward-looking guidance

- Consider analysts' expectations for company performance

13 | *Correspondence with securities regulators*

It is common for securities regulators to review a company's financial filings and to question certain accounting or disclosures. Regulators then provide a document often referred to as a "comment letter," and the company typically has to respond within a relatively short time frame. If regulators don't consider the response to be satisfactory, the company may have to answer additional questions. In serious cases, regulators require companies to amend or restate previous filings (which can lead to litigation and other adverse consequences, as discussed in Chapter 6). Consequently, it is important for audit committees to understand the nature of such inquiries and be familiar with the company's responses. Plus, in the United States, the SEC publicly discloses these comment letters as well as companies' responses.

Astute audit committees review the comment letter as well as a draft of management's proposed responses, which generally have been discussed with the external auditors.

SEC comment letters frequently question:

- Segment reporting
- Impairment testing
- Uncertain tax positions
- Valuation allowances against deferred tax assets
- Classification of items in the statement of cash flows

- Derivatives valuations
- Pension obligations
- Revenue recognition
- Early-warning disclosures

A company can respond to comment letters most easily if it had prepared documentation at the time management originally determined the accounting. This documentation usually proves more compelling than documentation the company prepares after its regulator has expressed concerns.

Management can also be proactive in dealing with securities regulators. If there is some uncertainty or dispute as to whether a proposed accounting method is appropriate, the company can submit its proposed accounting to the regulators in writing, with its rationale — effectively asking for a "preclearance letter." The regulators will ask for the external auditors' view of the appropriate accounting, if it is not provided in the submission. Given the sensitivity of these situations, the audit committee should be aware of such outreach and concur with the approach the company is planning.

14 | Timing issues

Companies issue press releases containing preliminary results to get earnings information into the market. The company's stock price typically reacts to these preliminary disclosures — which may be released long before the financial statements are filed. In fact, this interval can be several weeks, as shown in Exhibit 1.7. During this period, management will finalize the financial statements and footnote disclosures and the auditors will finish their work.

Exhibit 1.7	Example financial reporting schedule for a large company
Year end	December 31
First close of general ledger	January 6
Post close adjusting entries booked	January 8
Final close of general ledger	January 9
First draft of financial statements available for management review	January 12
Final draft of financial results	January 14
Audit committee review of preliminary results press release	January 18
Issuance of preliminary results press release	January 19
Finalization of financial statements with footnotes and disclosures	February 14
Audit committee approval of issuance	February 15
Issuance/filing of financial statements	February 16

But the intervening period between press release and filing presents a risk that other significant events may occur, some of which could require management to change previously released earnings. Because financial statement users rely on preliminary results, companies are extremely reluctant to revise those results when they finalize their financial statements. Furthermore, even if an event doesn't require the company to retroactively change results, securities regulators have increasingly been insisting that companies disclose such developments contemporaneously.

Accounting standards address how companies should deal with events that occur after year end but before the financial statements are filed. Some types of subsequent events represent additional information regarding management's assumptions that was not available at year end. In many cases, these events require management to adjust the year-end balances because they either validate or further clarify facts and circumstances that existed at the balance sheet date. Such events can present challenges for both management and audit committees and, in some cases, their existence may affect the date of the company's earnings release or when it finalizes and files its full financial statements.

Exhibit 1.8 provides examples of the type of information that could require the company to amend the results included in a press release.

Exhibit 1.8	Subsequent events that could require a company to revise previously released earnings
• Settlement of a lawsuit or an offer made by the company to settle • Bankruptcy of a customer, indicating a reduced ability to pay • Actual customer returns that exceed the level anticipated • Notice from an environmental agency of a previously unrecorded claim	• Finalization of the audit of an open tax year by a taxing authority, finding a different amount payable than the estimate • Additional evidence obtained of an asset impairment • Further evidence of slow-moving or obsolete inventory

There are other types of subsequent events that don't relate to facts and circumstances that existed at the balance sheet date. Companies simply need to disclose these, rather than adjust their year-end balances. Making an acquisition or incurring new debt are examples of such events.

Because of stakeholders' interest in preliminary earnings releases, plus the potential embarrassment of having to revise those results for subsequent events, astute audit committees don't underestimate their importance. It is critical that management monitor events that occur subsequent to period end but before the full financial statements are issued.

For their part, audit committees should ask management about whether any such significant events occurred and what effect they had. More fundamentally, the possibility that these type of events could occur may even cause the company to reconsider the timing of the earnings release or the filing date.

2

Risk Management and the System of Internal Control

Companies face numerous risks, including strategic, operational, and environmental risks. Boards generally have the responsibility to oversee risk management, as discussed at greater length in *Board Effectiveness — What Works Best,* 2nd edition. Although audit committees rarely have responsibility to oversee all the risks in a company, they do commonly oversee those relating to financial reporting, fraud, compliance with laws and regulations, information technology, and privacy. It is important for audit committees to understand the extent of their risk oversight responsibilities versus those assigned to the entire board or other committees.

Internal controls should reduce risk exposures to a level that is consistent with the company's risk appetite. In many countries, public companies provide some form of reporting on internal controls or risk management, and audit committees are often involved in reviewing such reports.

Starting in 2010, U.S. companies have to disclose their boards' role in risk oversight. In a PwC analysis of the 2010 proxy disclosures of 100 major companies, the board as a whole was cited as being responsible for risk oversight for almost every company. However, the audit committee was nearly always noted as having a role in supporting the board in its risk oversight.

This chapter addresses:
1. Risk management processes
2. Internal controls
3. Incentives and fraud risk
4. Financial reporting fraud risk
5. Bribery and corruption risk

1 | *Risk management processes*

A robust process to manage risks helps a company achieve its performance and profitability targets. Ideally, such a process links risk management to company strategy and risk appetite, effectively identifies potential events that may affect the company, and mitigates risks that are at an unacceptable level. Internal control systems are designed to help companies mitigate known risks, and so audit committees' oversight of internal control and risk management is often intertwined.

Overseeing how management addresses risk for financial reporting is clearly in an audit committee's domain (and is discussed later in this chapter); however, some audit committees take broader responsibility for overseeing risk management.

Indeed, New York Stock Exchange rules require audit committees to discuss policies with respect to risk assessment and risk management. Although it is management's role to assess and manage the company's exposure to risk, the audit committee should be comfortable with the process management has implemented. Similarly, audit committees in India have the responsibility to review financial and risk management policies.

The Australian Stock Exchange's *Corporate Governance Principles and Recommendations* indicate that the audit committee should report to the board on the results of the committee's review of risk management and internal control systems.

There is a European Parliament directive calling on companies to report on their internal control and risk management systems. Accordingly, a number of countries have adopted laws that align with this directive. For example, in France one element of the board chair's report discusses internal control and risk management; audit committees typically assess that element of the report before it is approved by the board. In the Netherlands, the audit committee oversees the company's risk management and internal control systems.

In the United Kingdom, the Turnbull Guidance to the Combined Code on Corporate Governance recommends that, as a minimum, the board disclose that there is an ongoing process for identifying, evaluating, and managing the significant risks faced by the company. In addition, the board should disclose that the process has been in place for the entire year covered by the annual report and is regularly reviewed by the board. Audit committees, by the nature of their oversight, often play a key role in reviewing and approving these disclosures.

To provide a framework to assist companies with improving risk management, a number of organizations have issued relevant guidance. The two most prominent frameworks are by the Committee of Sponsoring Organizations of the Treadway Commission (COSO) with its *Enterprise Risk Management — Integrated Framework* and the risk management guidelines released by the International Organization for Standardization (ISO). Audit committees may wish to understand what guidance management is applying in its risk management activities.

Interview insights
The entire board is responsible for risk oversight, but the audit committee coordinates the process.
– AC Chair

Interview insights
The company's risk matrix changes over time, as some key risks are added and others are dropped. If we identify any other risks, management considers adding them to the matrix like they would consider risks submitted from any other part of the business.
– IA Director

With audit committees already having significant responsibilities, many audit committee chairs and other observers are deeply concerned about charging audit committees with full responsibility for overseeing risk management. They argue that audit committees already have overly-full plates. But while audit committees generally are not charged with overseeing all the risks that a company faces, many do take on the responsibility to oversee the process that management uses.

Those audit committees that have responsibility for overseeing the risk management process likely will want to:

- Understand how the process works
  - How management identifies events that could put the company at risk and how it assesses the likelihood and impact of identified risks
  - How management has tailored the process to meet the company's specific needs
  - Whether the process is continuous — not performed just at a single point in time
  - If the individual assigned primary responsibility for risk management has appropriate expertise, stature within the company, and available time

- Understand the top risks management has identified (sometimes referred to as a risk "heat map") and ensure these are communicated to the entire board as well

- Understand internal audit's role in risk management and the extent to which its audit plan covers the key risks

- Work with the other board committees to allocate oversight of key risks among board committees or to the full board — to ensure that all key risks are subject to board-level oversight

Though audit committees rarely oversee all key risks that are identified from the risk assessment process, they do take primary responsibility for overseeing how management monitors and controls the company's major financial risk exposures, including fraud risk. That often includes periodically meeting with the individuals who are responsible for identifying and managing such risks. It's key for the audit committee to be vigilant — and to avoid becoming overburdened by taking on responsibility to oversee more risks than it can handle, given all the other required items that pack its agenda.

2 | *Internal controls*

The system of internal control is essential to a successful risk management program. Internal controls can help mitigate risk exposures to an acceptable level.

Various countries have developed control frameworks to assist companies in designing and assessing controls. For example, in the United States, COSO published an integrated framework for internal control (see Exhibit 2.1), and Canada has the Criteria of Control framework.

Exhibit 2.1	COSO internal control — integrated framework

Internal control is a process that provides reasonable assurance a company will be able to achieve its objectives for:

- Effectiveness and efficiency of operations
- Reliability of financial reporting
- Compliance with applicable laws and regulations (as discussed in Chapter 3)

Framework components: control environment, risk assessment, information and communication, control activities, and monitoring of controls

It's not especially easy for an audit committee to understand whether the company has adequate internal controls. The extent of controls a company needs will vary depending on its size, sophistication, market, and the complexity of its business. Accordingly, necessary key controls may differ substantially from one company to another and from one industry to the next. For example, a financial institution will require more sophisticated controls than a company selling a single product or service in only one market. And so, audit committees will want to discuss with management whether the company's system of internal control is tailored to its individual profile and adequate under the circumstances.

The Sarbanes-Oxley Act requires U.S. public companies to report on internal control over financial reporting. *Companies must document, test, and evaluate these controls and provide a report that:*

- Acknowledges management's responsibility for establishing and maintaining adequate internal control over financial reporting
- Identifies the framework (e.g., the COSO framework) management used to evaluate controls
- Indicates management's conclusion regarding the effectiveness of those controls
- Describes any material weaknesses that exist

Requirements are similar in other countries such as India, where the CEO and CFO certify to the board that they accept responsibility for establishing, maintaining, and evaluating effectiveness of internal control over financial reporting.

While management is responsible for implementing effective internal control over financial reporting, audit committees should:

- Meet periodically with individuals who are primarily responsible for internal control over financial reporting

- Understand, and help set, the tone at the top (see discussion in Chapter 3)

- Discuss with management the controls in place to mitigate key financial reporting risks, including fraud risks

- Focus discussions on areas of greatest potential risk, such as those in Exhibit 2.2

- Understand how management plans to assess internal control and what role internal audit and other related resources will play

- Understand the external auditors' scope and plan to test the controls. (Larger U.S. public companies must have their external auditors attest to the effectiveness of the company's internal control over financial reporting.)

- Meet regularly with management, internal audit, and the external auditors to discuss status and findings — particularly significant deficiencies and material weaknesses — as well as management's action plan to respond appropriately

Exhibit 2.2	Areas of greatest potential risk for internal control over financial reporting

Management override of controls: Audit committees should carefully consider whether — and how — management could override established controls and what procedures mitigate this risk.

Outside service providers: Audit committees of companies that partly or wholly outsource key functions — such as recordkeeping, information systems processing, systems development, or internal control testing — should be comfortable that management is properly monitoring the outside service providers and ensuring their work is appropriate.

Information technology: Audit committees should consider whether their members have the knowledge, or can leverage internal or external experts, to oversee the complex information technology that underlies internal controls. Audit committees need to ask insightful questions regarding controls over integrity of customer data, privacy, security, and access. Plus, new technologies and developments

in areas such as social media and cloud computing pose both opportunities and risks that even management may not fully recognize.

Mergers and acquisitions: Audit committees should ask how management is considering the target company's internal controls when assessing such transactions. Due diligence should include specific consideration of the system of internal controls and its implications for external reporting requirements — specifically, the state of the target's internal control environment and the company's plans to merge operations and ability to standardize controls after acquisition.

Impact of restructuring: Reduced staffing levels, changes to the business model, consolidated operations, asset sales, and resulting changes to processes and information systems can significantly affect the control environment. Audit committees should inquire how management addresses the impact of such changes on internal control.

3 | *Incentives and fraud risk*

Regulators and shareholders are focusing on the link between compensation and risk in companies — particularly whether incentives may prompt executives and employees to take unacceptable operational risks. Audit committees focus more on the extent to which incentives may encourage fraudulent financial reporting.

Indeed, the PwC *2009 Global Economic Crime Survey* found a linkage between executive compensation structures and increased risk. Companies that base more than 50% of senior executive compensation on performance (i.e., variable pay components) reported fraud at a higher level than companies that did not (36% versus 20%).

Ideally, compensation committees design compensation packages that promote ethical behavior without compromising long-term shareholder value. Astute audit committees question the extent to which incentives could create risk for financial reporting. *And they understand the need to consider the risk associated with compensation plans by:*

- Developing a robust understanding of compensation programs. Some committees do so through one or more of the following:

  - Having cross-committee membership between the compensation committee and the audit committee

  - Holding periodic meetings between the audit committee and the compensation committee

  - Inviting the compensation committee chair to periodically meet with the audit committee

- Understanding financial targets incorporated in compensation programs and the degree to which compensation changes if the targets are met

Interview insights
The audit committee needs to understand compensation schemes to be able to fully understand bonus thresholds.
– AC Chair

Interview insights
In all my companies, the audit committee and the compensation committee have overlapping membership. This is important, especially when there is pay for performance.
– AC Chair

4 | *Financial reporting fraud risk*

Interview insights

There is a dedicated internal audit unit for compliance issues. This unit performs preventive audits and investigates all potential instances of fraud. At our company, we take compliance very seriously.

– IA Director

The Association of Certified Fraud Examiners' *2010 Report to the Nations on Occupational Fraud and Abuse* covered survey results from more than 100 countries. It concluded that asset misappropriations (where employees steal or misuse an organization's resources) are the most common form of fraud, followed by corruption (where an employee gains a personal benefit by violating his or her duty to the company, including bribery, extortion, and conflicts of interest). Though financial statement fraud is less common, it has a much greater financial impact, the report found.

Weaknesses in internal control can make companies more susceptible to fraud. There are many types of fraud, including misappropriation of company assets, insider trading, and bribery. But the type of fraud that is of grave concern for audit committees is financial reporting fraud.

Financial reporting fraud is commonly defined as a deliberate misrepresentation of a company's financial position, stemming from intentional misstatements or omissions in the financial statements.

Many high-profile companies around the world have admitted to fraudulent financial reporting. In doing so, they damaged investor confidence and experienced other adverse consequences, as discussed in Chapter 6. Consequently, securities regulators place tremendous emphasis on preventing and detecting fraud. So management needs to set the proper tone at the top; maintain high ethical standards; and establish appropriate controls to prevent, deter, and detect fraud.

Auditing standard setters share the concern about fraud. Auditing standards throughout the world typically require auditors to gain reasonable assurance that the financial statements are not materially misstated as a result of fraud. And audit committees, for their part, are commonly expected to play a key role in reducing fraud risk as part of their oversight of financial reporting.

Fraud is a pervasive problem — 38% of respondents to the PwC *2009 Global Economic Crime Survey* reported their companies had experienced accounting fraud the prior year. So why does financial reporting fraud continue, despite the damage it can create? The Center for Audit Quality in the United States issued a 2010 report, *Deterring and Detecting Financial Reporting Fraud*. **Among the most common motivators for financial reporting fraud cited:**

- To meet analysts' earnings expectations
- For personal gain, including maximizing bonuses and compensation
- To conceal bad news, such as the company's deteriorating financial condition

- To increase the company's stock price
- To bolster financial performance, for a pending equity offering or debt financing

When these pressures are present, audit committees need to consider the potential for increased fraud risk. And if the company is in a challenging economic environment, these risks may be exacerbated.

Other factors can contribute to higher fraud risk: transfer of operations to new locations, particularly in developing markets; significant restructurings and reductions in workforce; reductions in the scope of internal audit's work; and the industry in which the company operates. The PwC *2009 Global Economic Crime Survey* indicates that the communications, insurance, financial services, and hospitality and leisure industries reported having experienced the most economic crimes.

Once the audit committee understands any factors increasing fraud risk, it's better equipped to properly oversee the internal controls related to fraud detection.

Fundamentally, maintaining skepticism about the risk of fraud at a company is tough to do. Directors wouldn't serve on a board if they didn't trust management. But fraud does happen, and so audit committees in particular need to be alert for it. How can they do that? Exhibit 2.3 highlights selected considerations for audit committees, stemming from the Center for Audit Quality report.

Exhibit 2.3	Considerations for audit committees in preventing fraud

- Oversee any aspects of the company's strategy that affect financial reporting
- Focus on the risks that could create incentives for financial reporting fraud
- Assess management integrity regularly
- Review and understand the results of complaints to the whistleblower hotline
- Fully understand related party transactions and significant nonroutine transactions
- Have management periodically report on the control environment and fraud prevention programs

Audit committees also address the risk of fraud by assessing the tone at the top and overseeing the company's compliance program and whistleblower program, as discussed in Chapter 3.

5 | Bribery and corruption risk

Bribery and corruption are significant and growing risks for companies. PwC's *2009 Global Economic Crime Survey* indicates that 27% of companies reported they had experienced bribery or corruption. The Association of Certified Fraud Examiners *2010 Report to the Nations on Occupational Fraud and Abuse* found corruption fraud present in 33% of the more than 1,800 fraud cases covered in the survey. Adding to the risks in this area, enforcement agencies around the world are not only pursuing corruption more vigilantly, but also are working together to do so.

Accordingly, companies need robust control systems to mitigate the risk of bribery and corruption. But PwC's 2008 report, *Confronting Corruption* found that while 80% of respondents say they have an anticorruption program, only 22% are confident that it mitigates corruption risks. Only 50% say their program is clearly communicated and enforced, and only 40% believe their controls identify high-risk business partners or suspicious disbursements. Plus, when PwC's *2010 Annual Corporate Directors Survey* asked about their companies' program for compliance with the Foreign Corrupt Practices Act (FCPA), 25% of the directors indicated their companies didn't have such a program.

Clearly, there is work to do.

The FCPA, passed in 1977, sets requirements for companies in the United States. It prohibits companies from offering, promising to pay, authorizing, or giving anything of value to a foreign official to influence the official to give the company an improper advantage. Such payments are barred under any circumstance, whether they are made directly or indirectly, through a third party, or to a third person for the benefit of the official. Since the conduct of third parties — including foreign agents, distributors, consultants, and business partners — could expose a company to FCPA violations, companies need controls to cover such relationships.

The FCPA also requires companies to keep accurate records of transactions and to maintain a system of internal control to provide reasonable assurance that transactions are authorized and recorded. Because the FCPA doesn't recognize a materiality concept, the risk of violations is significant and difficult to manage.

The amount of any fines for violating the FCPA can be of concern. When a violation is detected, a company often is compelled to conduct an investigation — which can involve significant costs and take years to complete. The company may have to extend the investigation to other jurisdictions in which the company operates to confirm that improper behavior is not pervasive.

The other challenge is that in mergers and acquisitions, the acquiring company may become liable for FCPA violations for the operations it buys. So audit committees will want to be comfortable that management has FCPA due diligence as an integral part of the merger and acquisition checklist.

Although few FCPA cases were brought in the law's first 25 years, at the end of 2010, more than 150 cases were open.

And while audit committees are concerned about the FCPA, other developments also merit attention. The U.K. Bribery Act of 2010 is broader than the FCPA. The U.K. act prohibits facilitating payments to anyone, not just to government officials. It allows individuals to be sentenced for up to 10 years in prison and doesn't limit fines against companies. It also requires companies to put systems and controls in place to support compliance. It is scheduled to take effect in 2011 and applies to any company with operations in the United Kingdom.

The Dodd-Frank Act of 2010 directs the U.S. Securities and Exchange Commission to compensate whistleblowers (by sharing a portion of company fines) for reporting corrupt activity, as discussed further in Chapter 3. This change is expected to significantly increase the number of bribery and corruption allegations, which may compel companies to conduct a greater number of investigations.

One helpful starting point for audit committees that are trying to understand the level of bribery and corruption risk in their companies, given the legislative focus, is to assess whether their companies are operating in regions and industries that are more susceptible to corruption. These are shown in Exhibit 2.4.

Interview insights

The committee is alert to the risks and challenges from operating in (our country) — illicit payments and circumvention and override of controls.

– AC Chair

Exhibit 2.4	Countries and industries with higher risks of bribery and corruption

Countries:		Industries:
• Somalia • Myanmar • Afghanistan • Iraq • Uzbekistan	• Turkmenistan • Sudan • Chad • Burundi • Equatorial Guinea	• Real estate and property development • Oil and gas • Heavy manufacturing • Mining • Pharmaceutical and medical care

Source: Transparency International. Country list relates to public sector corruption, per 2010 Corruption Perceptions Index. Industry list from 2008 Bribe Payers Index.

Once they understand the overall risk level, audit committees should focus on how management is minimizing the risks of bribery and corruption fraud to protect the company's reputation and reduce its exposure to financial penalties. Is the CEO setting the right ethical tone and culture?

Additionally, audit committees may wish to ask management whether compliance programs specifically address the FCPA and other anti-bribery legislation and whether programs are tailored to incorporate:

- *Risk analysis:* Covering all aspects of the business, including countries of operation and type of business, and updated to respond to new business approaches or to exposures in new territories. Making FCPA due diligence an integral part of acquisitions.

- *Training:* Specifically targeting employees and relevant third parties (such as agents) in compliance-sensitive positions and conducted locally, with emphasis on the FCPA for "riskier" locations.

- *Sanctions:* Determining, communicating, and enforcing consequences for policy violations.

- *Monitoring:* Involving the legal department in preapproving agents and distributors. Higher-risk transactions such as travel and entertainment, marketing and consulting fees, gifts, and charitable and political contributions should be monitored regularly. Sales commissions and discounts should also be reviewed, and government contracts should be identified, segregated, and tracked.

- *Auditing:* Conducting regular audits of agent commissions, distributor discounts, or finder's fee payments.

- *Assistance:* Giving employees access to advice on how to report potential violations.

3

Culture and Compliance — the Soul of Corporate Accountability

Many audit committees oversee the tone at the top, understanding that having effective internal controls depends greatly on the company's culture. Company culture is also key to the effectiveness of compliance and ethics programs. Such programs must be designed to shape an environment that encourages employees to comply with applicable laws and regulations, and to promote proper behavior across the entire company.

Directors generally recognize their responsibility to oversee ethics. The National Association of Corporate Directors' *2010 Public Company Governance Survey* indicates that 77% of boards evaluate management's ethics.

This chapter addresses audit committee involvement in an effective corporate compliance and financial reporting culture:

1. Tone at the top
2. Compliance and ethics programs
   i. Codes of conduct
   ii. Conflicts of interest
   iii. Whistleblower and complaint hotlines

1 | *Tone at the top*

Tone at the top is about creating a culture where everyone feels responsible for doing the right thing. The company's top executives need to consistently reinforce this message. If employees see an executive acting in an inappropriate or unethical way, they may feel justified doing the same. But it's even more important that middle management reinforces the right tone, as surveys suggest this "message in the middle" has a greater influence on how employees conduct themselves. Employees often point to consistent and frequent communication about ethics as being important, though many feel management's message could be more impactful.

While boards overall are responsible for overseeing the tone at the top (see *Board Effectiveness — What Works Best,* 2nd edition), audit committees often play a key role. Their challenge is to discern whether the tone that management communicates to the committee is really the tone that permeates the entire company.

How can committees evaluate what the tone at the top really is? First, use the committee's direct interaction with executives and managers to assess their personal attributes and ethical stature. This is certainly the most common way committees judge the financial reporting culture. Then, consider additional ways to evaluate the tone at the top.

One possible approach is to review a summary of employee surveys. Surveys can provide valuable feedback and insight regarding the company's ethical culture, especially when they cover a broad base of employees. While such surveys often address employee satisfaction or working conditions, they can also ask questions that address whether employees have faced pressure to bend the rules and whether they think their managers are willing to do so. The percentage of participation in such surveys may also send a message about the compliance culture.

> *Interview insights*
> Tone at the top is easy to judge if it's at the extremes — either very good or very bad. It's tougher when the tone is somewhere in the middle.
> – AC Chair

Interview insights

From a practical perspective, assessing the tone at the top is difficult as a stand-alone exercise. We very much base it on a holistic assessment of numerous factors (e.g., formal and informal meetings, reviews of reports, watching management's actions).

– AC Chair

Another way to evaluate the tone at the top is to ask the human resources department about upward feedback that executives and managers receive from their direct reports. The results of such evaluations, particularly from employees in the controllership group, can shed light on inappropriate pressure being placed on financial reporting personnel. Having middle management finance personnel periodically meet with the committee can also provide insight.

Additionally, monitoring the level of employee complaints, including the whistleblower hotline (discussed later in this chapter), helps the committee gain perspective into ethical culture. Committees also should ask internal auditors and external auditors about their perceptions. Such discussions can be held during private sessions or ad hoc conversations when management is not present. See further discussion of executive or private sessions with auditors in Chapters 4 and 5.

2 | Compliance and ethics programs

Many of a company's stakeholders view compliance and ethics broadly — as going beyond mere compliance with laws and regulations. Board directors should understand how issues such as corporate responsibility and sustainability affect the company's ethical reputation. Given how strategic some of these issues are, often a special board committee or the entire board may take oversight responsibility for them, as discussed in *Board Effectiveness — What Works Best,* 2nd edition.

In addition to these evolving stakeholder expectations about what constitutes ethical behavior, companies face increasingly complex operating environments, as they need to track and comply with numerous and changing laws and regulations. A company's compliance program usually goes hand in hand with its code of ethics. The company's compliance and ethics program is a subset and part of the overall system of internal controls, which is discussed in Chapter 2.

In the United States, the Federal Sentencing Guidelines (the guidelines) establish base-level expectations for compliance and ethics programs. All companies that conduct business in the United States are covered by the guidelines. One reason these are important to companies is because the guidelines permit judges to reduce fines if a company is convicted of felonies and certain misdemeanors but can show that it has an effective compliance and ethics program. The guidelines also allow judges to reduce fines if companies self-report, cooperate, or accept responsibility.

The guidelines say that, for a company to be considered to have an "effective" compliance and ethics program, it has to exercise due diligence to prevent and detect criminal conduct and otherwise promote a culture that encourages ethical conduct and commitment to compliance with the law. *The guidelines were revised in 2010 and emphasize the need:*

- To use reasonable efforts before hiring or promoting individuals who will have substantial discretionary authority, to ensure they haven't engaged in illegal activities or other inappropriate conduct

- To establish standards and procedures to prevent and detect criminal conduct

- To conduct training about the program

- To take reasonable steps to ensure the compliance and ethics program is followed, by monitoring activities to detect criminal conduct, periodically evaluating the program's effectiveness, and having and advertising an anonymous hotline for employees to report issues or seek guidance

- To take reasonable steps after criminal conduct has been detected to respond appropriately and prevent further similar conduct

- For the board to be knowledgeable about the content and operation of the program and to exercise reasonable oversight with respect to its implementation and effectiveness

- For the individual who is responsible for the program to have direct access to the board or a board committee and to report periodically to that body on the effectiveness of the program

In many countries, case law establishes expectations for board involvement with compliance programs. Such precedents direct boards to ensure that reporting systems exist to provide senior management and the board with timely, accurate information on the company's compliance with laws. In countries such as the Netherlands, the board is specifically charged with overseeing the company's compliance with legislation and regulation. Directors may even have an affirmative duty (as they do in the United States) to determine whether the company has an effective compliance program.

The "compliance officer" role is often established separately — particularly in larger companies — rather than being assumed by the general counsel or CFO. One issue is determining which function the compliance officer should report through — legal, finance, internal audit, risk, operations, or other. Many companies have decided to have the compliance officer report through the legal function, recognizing the legal nature of many compliance issues. Others, though, choose another reporting structure, as they view ethics and compliance as a business issue, not simply a legal one.

Audit committees often are given responsibility for overseeing the compliance and ethics program. The New York Stock Exchange rules require the audit committee to oversee the company's compliance with legal and regulatory requirements. In other companies, even if another board committee monitors compliance, the audit committee still needs to understand any major compliance issues so that it can consider the financial statement impact.

Audit committees can oversee and support the effectiveness of compliance programs by:

- Understanding the design of the company's compliance program, including areas of higher risk, the key personnel involved and their backgrounds, reporting lines, challenges, and approaches to addressing specific major requirements

- Discussing the effectiveness of the program

- Reviewing the ethics policy periodically and understanding how it is communicated to employees and how it addresses the risk that ethical standards differ from country to country

- Meeting periodically with the compliance officer to discuss the function's independence and resources

- Understanding the nature of any significant issues that come to light (whether identified by the company or by regulators), management's investigation, and any follow-up or disciplinary actions.

- Being satisfied management is making any changes required to ensure ongoing program effectiveness

Understanding how internal audit assesses the risks inherent in the compliance and ethics program and covers them in audit plans can help the audit committee with its oversight. First, as an objective third party, internal audit can provide a sound independent check on the program's effectiveness. Second, internal audit typically has more resources than the compliance group and already reaches across the entire company.

Audit committees should get periodic briefings and information from the internal audit director, general counsel, compliance officer, and management on the state of compliance and any significant issues. Exhibit 3.1 provides a list of what elements such reports may provide.

Exhibit 3.1	Typical items covered in a report on a company's compliance program

- An incident management log

- Narrative discussion of escalated incidents

- Analysis of the incident (topic, location, business unit, level of personnel, etc.)

- Statistics on code of conduct training and certifications

- Trends of incidents reported over time

- Results of employee surveys on compliance and ethics

- Planned actions relative to identified issues

i. Codes of conduct

Many companies establish codes of conduct to communicate expectations about acceptable business practice to all employees. Generally, codes of conduct are available on a company's website. Indeed, rules in the United States require public companies to adopt and make their codes available to the public. Similarly, the Australian Stock Exchange Corporate Governance Council's Principles of Good Corporate Governance and Best Practice Recommendations encourage companies to adopt and disclose a code of conduct to guide directors and executive management on ethical matters relating to financial integrity. In South Africa, the King Report recommends the board develop a code of conduct, which should be regularly reviewed and updated as necessary. Brazil's Institute of Corporate Governance Code calls for the audit committee to see that the company's code of conduct is enforced. In India, the code of conduct is posted on the company's website; board directors and senior management affirm their compliance with the code in the annual report.

A code of conduct is a proactive statement of the company's expectations for employee and corporate conduct. Companies should tailor their codes to meet their individual needs and culture.

Although codes can cover various topics, at a minimum they should affirm:

- Expectations for professional behavior at, and outside, the workplace when conducting company business

- Employees' responsibilities for reporting misconduct or expressing concerns

- Standards of responsibility both for management and nonmanagement employees

- A specific process for disciplinary actions when policy violations are discovered. Depending on the severity of the violation, the process may include a verbal warning, a written warning, corrective actions, follow-up review and report, or finally, dismissal.

- The fact that some management and senior employees may be held personally and/or criminally liable for their own actions

Codes of conduct also typically address conflicts of interest; corporate opportunities; confidentiality; fairness; protection and use of company assets; honesty; integrity; compliance with laws, rules, and regulations; and accountability for adherence to the code. A code should also address any policy issues critical to the company's industry.

The audit committee should look to see the company has adopted a code of conduct and whether the company is effectively communicating it to employees and training them. The committee will also want to understand the extent to which employees have certified they have read and are complying with the code.

Astute committees also recognize that developing and adopting a code may be more challenging for multinational companies. The implementation challenges that often arise include language translation issues, differences in local laws, and differing expectations for minimum behavior in different geographies. As a consequence, many companies supplement their global code of conduct with country-specific guidance to address local business environments. And they stress that employees must go beyond the requirements of the written code if higher ethical standards exist where those employees conduct business.

ii. Conflicts of interest

Codes of conduct often incorporate conflict of interest policies. Such policies typically cover financial conflicts, outside employment or business interests, employees who are related to each other, indirect interests and relationships, gifts and entertainment, protection and use of confidential information, and corporate opportunities. Developing a good conflict of interest policy can be challenging, especially to ensure it properly addresses culturally sensitive issues. For example, business practices in some cultures represent time-honored, noncorrupt traditions but appear to pose conflicts when viewed from American or European perspectives. The company may need to implement its policy differently for different cultures.

Exhibit 3.2 provides additional leading practices for conflict of interest policies.

The conflict of interest policies often have detailed provisions regarding executive and senior management-level conflicts and the procedures for granting and monitoring waivers. Many potential conflicts of interest, such as transactions between the company and entities where directors, officers, and executives have personal or professional interests, can trigger disclosures as related party transactions, as discussed in Chapter 1.

The responsibility for reviewing potential conflicts of interest can be assigned to various functions within the company. Based on the Society of Corporate Secretaries & Governance Professionals' *2008 Current Board Practices, Sixth Study,* the general counsel, followed by a board committee, was most likely to be responsible for reviewing potential conflicts of interest and related party transactions. In many cases, this obligation falls on the audit committee.

Exhibit 3.2	Leading practices for conflict of interest policies

Policy best practices: A good conflict of interest policy should:	*Process best practices: A good conflict of interest process should:*
• Be written	• Have the expressed support of top executives
• Be easy to obtain and understand	• Periodically assess whether it requires updating
• Be sufficiently general so as to cover potential conflicts not specifically mentioned by the policy	• Be publicized internally, especially following changes
• Include conflicts that represent key risks to the company and its industry	• Involve honest communication (for example, an acknowledgment from a top executive explaining what he or she had to do to comply with the policy)
• Pertain both to real and apparent conflicts	• Consistently enforce the policy
• Include questions and answers	• Establish appropriate protocols for waivers
• Apply to everyone, including board directors	• Support the policy with an annual certification process
• Be accompanied by disciplinary guidelines	• Cover the policy in ethics and/or compliance training
	• Involve a process for asking questions and reporting problems or violations

Audit committees (and all directors) should be familiar with the conflict of interest policy and their role in approving any waivers. And similar to the ethics policy, committees will want to understand whether the company has effectively communicated and trained its employees.

iii. Whistleblower and complaint hotlines

Audit committees have other sources of information about possible issues in a company, including "whistleblower" hotlines. Such programs have been used historically to identify inappropriate behavior on the part of company personnel, involving issues such as sexual harassment or violations of anti-bribery programs.

Many experts believe that providing a mechanism to allow employees to report concerns anonymously is core to compliance programs.

Indeed, the Sarbanes-Oxley Act of 2002 requires audit committees of U.S. public companies to establish procedures for the receipt, retention, and resolution of any complaints regarding accounting, internal accounting controls, or auditing matters — including procedures for employees' confidential, anonymous submissions. In Canada, Canadian Securities Administrators' rules mandate that audit committees establish procedures for receiving complaints and confidential concerns.

But the story is not that simple. In parts of the European Union, data protection regulations prohibit companies from implementing whistleblowing procedures that encourage anonymous reporting. And other regions, such as the United Kingdom, encourage — but don't require — whistleblower arrangements.

Countries that require direct audit committee involvement in whistleblower programs believe it will decrease the likelihood that managers who engage in wrongdoing will be able to suppress staff concerns over the long term.

It is important that information about whistleblower complaints be reported periodically to the audit committee. Some committees get a summary of all complaints received at least annually. Some also meet privately with the compliance officer to understand not only the nature, but also the frequency and trends of complaints reported to the hotline.

Audit committees should determine how often and at what level of detail they wish to receive information. Many committees find it useful to:

- Define a threshold (dollar value or level of management) for immediate reporting to the committee
- Review significant allegations periodically — say, quarterly
- Receive a summary of all allegations at least annually
- Have access to additional information

The Dodd-Frank Act of 2010 provides significantly enhanced whistleblower incentives and protections in the United States. It allows a whistleblower to be eligible for a reward of up to 30% of funds collected for providing original information to the U.S. Securities and Exchange Commission that leads to a fine of more than $1 million. The act also improves whistleblower protections preventing companies from retaliating against informants. Companies should ensure that internal whistleblower systems are effective because whistleblower activity on all fronts likely will be on the rise.

Audit committees will want to understand how management is modifying the company's code of conduct and other policies, if needed, to reflect the whistleblower rules from the Dodd-Frank Act.

4

Oversight of Management and Internal Audit

Balancing their role as management advisor with their fiduciary oversight duty is, to say the least, challenging for some audit committees. They need to carefully review information management provides and challenge it when appropriate. They must avoid, though, stepping into management's role.

The audit committee must also effectively oversee and support internal audit. Internal audit's role has changed over time, shifting focus between controls compliance and value-added consulting. Audit committees need to be satisfied with whatever roles internal auditors take on, given how valuable internal audit can be in providing objective assurance and insights to a committee.

A strong relationship with management and internal audit provides the essential foundation for the committee to effectively carry out its responsibilities.

This chapter discusses:

1. Overall relationship with management
2. Management bench strength
3. Meeting with management
4. Defining internal audit's role
5. Internal audit plans
6. Understanding internal audit resources
7. Communicating audit results
8. Internal audit reporting lines
9. Internal audit leadership
10. Private sessions
11. Evaluating internal audit's performance

1 | *Overall relationship with management*

Management has deep insight into the company and its challenges, and therefore is best positioned to recommend what information the audit committee needs. Management also marshals and prioritizes the resources and training that are essential to the committee effectively discharging its responsibilities. The support flows both ways. The committee can add value for management by bringing an objective perspective on financial reporting decisions and counseling on how to handle difficult issues.

Although audit committees should have a positive, trusting relationship with management, they need to maintain their skepticism and be ready to question management about uncomfortable topics, including fraud risk and the appropriateness of judgments. Management should expect rigorous questioning from the audit committee. If management doesn't provide clear responses or is overly defensive, that should raise a red flag for the committee. Exhibit 4.1 provides questions the audit committee can use to initiate such discussions, many of which are drawn from the 2010 Center for Audit Quality Report, *Deterring and Detecting Financial Reporting Fraud*.

> *Interview insights*
>
> Having active communications with management outside the committee meetings allows us to have a good understanding of issues as they arise.
>
> – AC Chair

Exhibit 4.1	Questions to ask company management about financial reporting

- Were there any transactions during the reporting period that would not have been entered into except to impact the company's financial ratios or presentation of results?

- Were there any transactions recorded during the last few weeks of the period that did not occur earlier in the period?

- Were any significant exceptions reported in the internal representation letters regarding financial reporting that are signed by various managers throughout the company?

- What judgment calls were required during the period? What was the decision process?

- What kind of input into accounting determinations does nonfinancial management have?

- What areas present recurring challenges or problems?

- If an article were to appear in *The Wall Street Journal* or the *Financial Times* about the company's accounting practices, what would it most likely talk about?

- What keeps you up at night?

- What areas of accounting require the most finance personnel time?

- What pressures influence financial reporting?

Conflict may arise when no clear understanding and consensus exist on where management's responsibilities end and the audit committee's begin. Management may believe it is doing its job by informing the committee of decisions made, whereas the committee may feel it should have been consulted in advance. Or the committee may provide perspectives on an item about which management did not request input. Whatever the source of conflict, such situations create dissatisfaction and even resentment — although typically unarticulated.

Accordingly, management should seek the committee's input when making key decisions and promptly inform the committee chair when significant issues arise. If the committee sees this communication is lacking, it needs to clarify its expectations with management, ideally as part of a private conversation. Periodically affirming which types of transactions the committee wants to have deeper involvement with may also be helpful.

Although committees have the right to ask for whatever information they feel they need, experienced committees respect the oversight role. They guard against requesting information about relatively minor matters or asking for it to be formatted to personal preferences.

The degree of interaction and involvement the committee has with management shifts with changes in the business environment, changes in the company's circumstances, and the capabilities of individuals in the finance function. So when the company is running in a steady state, the committee continues to review information carefully — and challenge management when necessary — but properly relies on management to resolve everyday issues.

2 | *Management bench strength*

Given the complexity of financial reporting, the work of a knowledgeable and technically competent finance team is vital to an audit committee's faith in the financial reports it reviews. And so, the audit committee should understand the skill, competency, and adequacy of resources on the finance team. How does an effective committee assess the strengths and performance of key finance managers and the broader finance team?

First, it discusses with the CFO how he or she ensures the finance team is appropriately qualified — and how the staff stays current with changing accounting standards. For a multinational company, the audit committee recognizes that the difficulty of the CFO's job is magnified, with the need to assure the competency of multiple finance teams that may have to apply more than one set of accounting standards. The committee also should understand how much influence head office finance has in selecting and directing those resources.

Second, the committee assesses how well senior finance personnel perform based on what it witnesses at committee meetings and how these employees respond to queries between meetings. Do they provide candid, understandable answers? Are they willing to admit when they need guidance or have to do further research before providing the answer? Do they appear to have a constructive working relationship with the external auditors?

Third, it considers the confidential feedback from internal and external auditors. That feedback can range from how well management understands and addresses technical accounting issues to whether management is setting the appropriate tone at the top by addressing significant control findings.

The audit committee will want to use private sessions of members only to conclude the evaluation of senior finance management's performance and the adequacy of the entire finance team.

An astute audit committee also monitors succession planning for the CFO position. The committee should discuss CFO succession with the CEO, especially if the current CFO will be retiring or moving elsewhere in the company. For CFO transitions, it's not unusual for the committee, or the chair, to interview a short list of candidates. Such involvement in the process helps the committee assure the incoming CFO will be comfortable reporting regularly and building a relationship with the chair, and that the candidate has ethics and integrity as well as financial reporting expertise.

Although management appointments often are viewed as the CEO's decision, the committee needs to be confident the incoming CFO is engaged and committed to portraying the company's results appropriately. Also, the audit committee's involvement reinforces with the incoming CFO that he or she has an important reporting responsibility to the committee and should anticipate the committee's needs, as well as responding to the CEO's requests.

Committees should consider being engaged in succession planning for the senior finance team, too. One way is to periodically discuss with the CFO how key finance team managers are being groomed for advancement.

Interview insights

Getting open and honest feedback in the private session from the external auditors is key in assessing the strength of management.

– AC Chair

3 | *Meeting with management*

Interview insights
We think it's vital to have an environment that encourages open dialogue and face-to-face discussions with management personnel from a wide cross section of the business throughout the year. We don't just rely on written reports.

– AC Chair

Formal and informal meetings with management are essential to a strong relationship. Of course, the main venue is the formal audit committee meetings. Management typically takes the lead in presenting on many agenda topics. But the aim is not simply to present at meetings. Management's participation should focus on engaging in meaningful dialogue with the committee, answering questions, and providing additional insight.

Which members of management should attend audit committee meetings? It would be hard for the audit committee to get the answers it needs without key members of the finance team present — the chief financial officer, chief accounting officer, and controller. Other senior finance personnel who may also have useful information to share include the tax director, treasurer, and chief information officer. If the committee is focusing on an issue at a business unit, then the presence of the business unit financial officer and controller might also be warranted. But numbers can quickly add up, and astute committee chairs know to control the number of "spectators" at meetings, as they can hamper committee discussions. And so if there is, for example, a tax topic on the agenda, the tax director will attend only that portion of the meeting.

A related question is whether the CEO should attend audit committee meetings. By and large, committee chairs believe the CEO's attendance is useful, as it helps ensure committee members' questions can be addressed on the spot. But knowledgeable chairs watch for any signs that the CEO's presence is dominating the meeting or impeding candid answers from other managers. And they ensure the CFO has time in private session with the committee to air any issues that he or she wasn't comfortable discussing in the full meeting.

Audit committees should regularly meet privately with the CFO. Private or executive sessions are appropriate to discuss sensitive matters, such as the considerations around the performance of the internal audit director and the external auditors. These sessions can also be an opportunity for a committee to find out if other developments or issues have surfaced that management believes the committee should be asking about or spending more time discussing.

To deepen their relationship, the audit committee chair and CFO should meet throughout the year informally. This not only provides the chair with better insight into the issues the company is dealing with, but also enables a stronger rapport between the CFO and the chair.

4 | *Defining internal audit's role*

A highly effective internal audit department can be an important resource, helping the committee understand how effectively the company is managing its business risks. Once the audit committee understands the work internal audit is performing, what other work it is capable of doing, and what management's objectives are for internal audit, the committee can reach consensus on what role internal audit should play to provide maximum value.

When first established, internal audit departments concentrated on assessing internal control compliance. In the 1990s, many internal audit functions shifted gears — becoming internal "consultants" to management in reengineering and process improvement efforts, with the goal of adding value. In the United States, the 2002 Sarbanes-Oxley Act caused internal audit to allocate significant resources to support management in documenting and testing internal control over financial reporting. With most companies needing fewer resources to perform their testing of financial reporting controls, internal audit has shifted focus to address other risks.

Internal audit can perform a wide variety of work. Exhibit 4.2 gives examples of the work internal auditors can do, on a spectrum from basic compliance to consulting, as well as the implications of such work.

Exhibit 4.2	Possible work internal audit could do
Type of work	Nature of work and implications
Assist in testing internal control over financial reporting/provide assistance to the external auditors	Traditional, compliance-oriented. Helps reduce costs.
On a rotational or risk ranked basis, audit the company's major operating units and functions (e.g., IT, payroll)	Traditional internal audit. That said, while audit has long covered major IT projects and security risks, the level, potential impact, and speed of change in these areas have increased substantially.
Perform legal and regulatory compliance audits; for example, health and safety audits	Greater internal audit role. Because of increased government regulation and a corresponding increase in risk, internal audit is providing more assurance that risks are being addressed and conducting related investigations.
Consult with management on process improvement and operational efficiency, especially related to major company initiatives, such as new products or entry into new markets	More consultative in nature and an area where internal audit's role is evolving. Nature of internal audit's work depends greatly on the skills it brings (e.g., supply chain or manufacturing excellence).

Interview insights
Internal audit could better assist the audit committee by covering the risks of new products and new processes in its work plan.

– AC Chair

Interview insights
People in the company don't understand the audit committee's expectations of internal audit. If the committee could articulate the importance of internal audit, that would elevate our role and importance.

– IA Director

In addition to planned audits and site visits, some internal audit departments use a continuous audit process which may involve ongoing control evaluations or risk assessments. This approach helps identify errors and fraud on a timely basis, and creates a stronger internal control environment across the company.

Often, different internal audit stakeholders see different value in different types of work by internal audit. The audit committee's challenge is to be comfortable internal audit is focusing its efforts in the right places and using its limited resources to provide not only value to management, but also assurance to the audit committee.

So what roles do internal audit functions typically fulfill? They usually cover areas such as assessing the company's key risks and how well they're mitigated; assessing IT security; and conducting investigations.

Internal audit's role should be reflected in its charter. A charter sets out internal audit's purpose, authority, reporting structure, and responsibilities and should specify the group cannot perform responsibilities that could hinder its objectivity. For example, it cannot be significantly involved in implementing internal controls it may have to test at a later time. Many audit committees review internal audit's charter annually, and approve any changes to the charter.

5 | *Internal audit plans*

Internal audit bases its annual audit plan on its risk assessment, which ideally should match up to key risks identified in the company's overall risk management program.

Internal audit's resources are not limitless. Therefore, it must make choices on which risks and operations it can cover in a given year, especially when faced with competing priorities between management's requests and the audit committee's expectations. Audit committees should review the planned scope of internal audit activities and understand how it responds to the level and types of risks within the company. Experienced committees understand that it's difficult for internal audit to drop audits of locations or functions it has historically performed annually, even if those audits no longer represent significant risk. And so committees should question the need to revisit locations or functions as regularly.

Committees also should understand there are some risk areas that few internal audit groups cover, and so likely won't be addressed in the audit plan. For instance, internal audit rarely helps companies assess risks around new product design, alignment to market needs, customer channel choice, or effectiveness of marketing programs. While these may represent significant risks to the company, they typically are not focus areas for the audit committee. Additionally, PwC's *2011 State of the Internal Audit Profession Study* shows that most internal audit functions are only marginally involved in risks associated with growth in emerging markets, cross-border acquisitions, new joint ventures, and new technologies such as cloud computing.

An internal audit plan may be appropriate at the time it was approved. But astute audit committees recognize that internal audit will need flexibility to respond to significant changes in the company — such as new product lines, global expansion, acquisitions, or unexpected regulatory issues. Indeed, some internal audit departments build "cushion" into their plan to address these unforeseen developments. Increasingly, internal audit also makes sure its audit plans are flexible so it can add or drop projects when risk priorities change.

As part of the annual plan discussion, audit committees should understand whether internal audit has an adequate budget to provide the right risk coverage and whether there are any constraints on internal audit's scope. The budget discussion should include the competitiveness of compensation levels, ability to seek expertise outside when it does not exist inside the company, appropriate use of technology, and training.

Most committees want to understand the degree to which internal audit's activities are coordinated with those of the external auditors. The goal should be to achieve effective and efficient audit coverage by the two groups. In situations where internal audit assists with external audit testing, the audit committee should inquire about whether the proportion of internal audit's work that is devoted to such assistance is appropriate.

As companies mature in other risk and compliance activities, it is also appropriate for the committee to ask how internal audit leverages assurance provided by the company's other risk or compliance functions such as risk management; credit or market risk; ethics and compliance; and environmental, health, and safety compliance.

Audit committees are not always involved in reviewing internal audit's plan. In such situations, the committee still should assess whether internal audit's work meets the committee's needs. If not, then the committee should reconsider its involvement in the audit planning process.

Interview insights
Our internal audit team needs to grow in conjunction with the rapid growth of our company. I tailor my staff recruiting plan based on the company's business plan.

– IA Director

6 | *Understanding internal audit resources*

Once the audit committee is satisfied with internal audit's plan, the next question is whether internal audit has the right resources, especially if the company's operations and strategy have increased complexity.

There are several ways to "staff" an internal audit function, and different approaches may affect the department's effectiveness. Some companies have their internal audit departments fully "in house." Others outsource most or all of the work. Many take a hybrid approach — using outside resources in selected circumstances to make the overall function stronger.

Interview insights
Not having the expertise in house doesn't mean we won't do an audit. We get the expertise.

– IA Director

Companies with fully "in-house" departments still face staffing model decisions. Some companies use rotational assignments, whereby individuals from finance and operations go "on tour" to the internal audit department for a period and then return to the business. A tour in internal audit can provide valuable training, giving the individual a better appreciation for risk and control and more insight into other areas of the company. Other internal audit departments use dedicated staff. Still others use a combined approach, with a mix of tour and core staff members.

Newly hired staff can bring needed technical skills and fresh perspectives. But a high turnover rate in internal audit can lead to staff or skill set shortages and a lack of "institutional memory" in the department. So internal audit should identify possible succession issues and periodically consider what new talent it needs to address any staff departures or shifts in the company's business model that mandate different audit skills.

One strategy some internal audit departments embrace is to outsource low-risk, routine work to allow internal audit more time to focus on strategic projects and key risks. Other internal audit directors use outsourcing to get access to specialty skills that allow the department to address highly complex risks.

The audit committee should understand the department's plans to address any resource or skill shortages. At times, it may make sense to "rent" those skills, although if done long term, the committee should be satisfied that is the right answer. From a strategic perspective, the committee also will want to oversee any decisions to more broadly outsource the internal audit function.

If the company outsources some or all of the internal audit function, the audit committee should understand the factors underlying that decision. Is it:

- To gain access to a wider range of skills and knowledge than a limited in-house department could support alone?

- To leverage specialist expertise (in areas such as information technology) that an individual internal audit department finds hard to retain or to keep current?

- To help cover audit requirements in foreign countries and bring knowledge of local business customs and languages?

If the company uses an outsource model to perform much or most of the internal audit plan, the committee should assure itself that the individuals who participate are qualified and objective and the service provider can ensure staff continuity. The same high expectations for internal audit quality should exist regardless of the resourcing model.

7 | Communicating audit results

Internal audit's interaction and communications with management and the audit committee greatly affect how the function is perceived. Positive perceptions are more likely if internal audit ties its work and findings to the company's business objectives and priorities.

Most internal audit departments issue numerous audit reports to management each year. Reports often include an overall grade for the audit as well as recommendations for management.

For its part, the audit committee should get a summary of the results of internal audit's work. Many internal audit groups struggle to get to the right level of detail in these reports, and consequently committees often have to review more information than needed. *Effective reports typically incorporate:*

- An executive summary that concisely describes the overall state of the company's control environment and sets the context for the rest of the report and for the discussion in the meeting. It should highlight any areas of significant concern.

- A description of internal audit's most significant findings, with business implications and indication of management's remediation plans.

- A listing of the results of all audits conducted since the last report, with the current rating and the prior rating for each audit and an indication of whether the control environment for that area or function is improving, deteriorating, or stable.

- The status of past significant audit recommendations, to allow the committee to monitor management's commitment to needed remediation and to understand if repeat issues exist, which can be a sign of an ineffective process.

The audit committee should expect internal audit's reports to be as professional as the information the committee receives from other parties. Some internal audit functions are particularly skillful at communicating needed information clearly and concisely. They use graphics and color to show trends. They focus on key points. And they provide effective analysis, not just raw detail. On any topic in the internal audit report, the head of internal audit should be able to answer the question "So what?"

Interview insights
Internal audit reports should contain only significant or critical matters; they shouldn't report on everything.

– AC Chair

8 | Internal audit reporting lines

Interview insights

The audit committee can help support internal audit's independence from management through the extent of its communications with internal audit and by making this level of engagement visible to management.

– AC Chair

The internal audit reporting level is important. It should demonstrate the highest support for internal audit's mandate, and it should support the function's objectivity. Often internal audit reports both to executive management (administratively) and to the audit committee.

The Institute of Internal Auditors' *1999 Global Audit Information Network* survey showed 43% of internal audit directors reported directly to the audit committee chair. Compare that to the *2010* survey, which shows 81% of internal audit directors report directly to the audit committee chair. Such a dramatic shift in only a decade demonstrates the understanding of how important it is for internal audit to be able to report issues to a supervisory body, not just to management.

As well as the direct line to the audit committee, internal audit usually reports administratively to management. Based on the Society of Corporate Secretaries & Governance Professionals' *2008 Benchmarking Survey Report*, 67% of internal auditors report to the CFO and 19% to the CEO.

The audit committee chair can reinforce the reporting relationship through periodic contact with the internal audit director between audit committee meetings. In major companies, sometimes this interaction is monthly. Easing the formality of reporting can help the committee ensure internal audit can provide timely reporting on operational or management issues that may arise. Plus, these meetings send the right tone-at-the-top message to internal audit and management.

9 | Internal audit leadership

Interview insights

The audit committee chair needs to have a good relationship with the internal audit director — it's a lonely job.

– AC Chair

The internal audit director drives the function's effectiveness and perception in the company. This person's background, experience, and executive presence play a key role in whether other executives view him or her as part of the management team and whether they hold internal audit in high regard.

The internal audit director walks a fine line, as a member of management and as the leader of an internal group that is expected to be objective of management. The committee and management need to be sensitive to this challenge and maintain ongoing dialogue with the director to learn quickly of any potential problems. The committee should expect the director to maintain an effective day-to-day working relationship with management, but also to have the courage to make tough calls when needed.

Lastly, succession planning is important to ensure that the transition to a new internal audit director is handled appropriately. Finding a candidate who has the right skill set and who the audit committee believes would be highly effective can be challenging. Typically both management and the audit committee play a role in the hiring of the internal audit director. And astute committee chairs know the importance of conducting an exit interview with the outgoing director to learn of any pertinent issues.

Audit committees should be involved in hiring the internal audit director, evaluating his or her performance, and being satisfied with that individual's compensation. Indeed, it appears many are. PwC's *2011 State of the Internal Audit Profession* research shows that 78% of audit committees play some role — ranging from having full involvement to providing input to management — in evaluating the internal audit director's performance and determining compensation.

10 | *Private sessions*

The audit committee should hold regular private meetings with the internal audit director, ideally at each in-person audit committee meeting. These private sessions should be scheduled as part of the agenda, and astute committee chairs preserve time for the sessions, even when other agenda items run over. Although it is more typical for the sessions to be held at the end of the meeting, some committees schedule them at the beginning so the committee can be alert to issues when the discussion arises. Committees also best support internal audit's objectivity when they insist that the private meetings occur and do not require the internal audit director to request the dialogue.

These private sessions allow more open and candid discussion than might otherwise occur with management present. They also allow the audit committee to derive the maximum benefit from its relationship with the internal audit director.

11 | *Evaluating internal audit's performance*

The audit committee can rely on internal audit's work and findings only if the function fulfills its duties. And so it's important the committee periodically discusses the department's effectiveness.

First, the committee should understand how internal audit monitors its own quality. Many departments at larger companies have quality assurance and improvement programs to check that audits are conducted in accordance with the department's standards, and with professional internal auditing standards. Many departments also have quality assessments done by external parties to conform with The Institute of Internal Auditors' *International Standards for the Professional Practice of Internal Auditing*. The *Standards* call for such assessments to be conducted at least every five years. The audit committee should understand the competency of the external reviewers and the results of both the internal and external quality assessments. The committee will also want to understand how internal audit is adjusting its work or processes to address major findings and areas for improvement.

Committees can also seek input from the external auditors. External auditors work with internal audit functions from different companies and can share a perspective on how well the department performs compared to others. Committees should also understand any red flags. For example, if the external auditors decide to place no reliance on internal audit's work or choose not to leverage any internal audit staff to assist with audit testing, the committee should understand why.

Discussions with the CFO and other members of management will provide additional views, including how internal audit is perceived throughout the company and whether the function approaches its work with a client service mentality.

Finally, the audit committee will have its own point of view through its interactions with internal audit.

There are also other factors the audit committee may want to probe.

- Is internal audit focused on the right topics?

- Does management turn to internal audit when there are issues?

- Is internal audit leveraging technology effectively, both to monitor for possible issues in the company and to make its own processes more efficient?

- Is internal audit issuing timely reports to management?

- Does internal audit have the right incentives — money and recognition — to drive superior performance?

5

Relationship with External Auditors

Audit committees play a key role in overseeing external auditors as part of the broader financial reporting process. Indeed, in a number of countries, audit committees take direct responsibility for the external audit relationship. Having the external auditors report directly to the committee, rather than to management, best positions the external auditors to raise contentious issues to the audit committee. Audit committees need an open, trusting, and professional relationship with the external auditors.

This chapter focuses on the essential ingredients for maximizing the value added by the external audit relationship in ensuring the integrity of a company's financial reporting processes. It covers:

1. The reporting relationship

2. Selection, reappointment, replacement, and evaluation of auditors

3. Auditor independence and objectivity

4. External audit scope

5. Audit fees

6. Communication of audit results and insights

7. Management representation letters

8. Private sessions

9. Disagreements with external auditors

10. Nonaudit services

11. Using other auditors

1 | *The reporting relationship*

External auditors should report directly to audit committees — not to, or through, management. In the United States, public companies' audit committees are directly responsible for appointing, retaining, compensating, and overseeing the work of external auditors, and the auditors report directly to the audit committees. Audit committees also must preapprove all audit (and nonaudit) services the external auditors provide to companies or their subsidiaries.

In the United Kingdom, the Combined Code on Corporate Governance states that one of the audit committee's main responsibilities is recommending to the board the appointment, reappointment, or removal of the external auditors and approving remuneration and terms of engagement. The code also recommends audit committees develop and implement a policy on external auditors providing nonaudit services. In Canada, the Canadian Securities Administrators recommend audit committees oversee external auditors, including their nomination and compensation. South African guidance states the audit committee should recommend to the board the appointment of the external auditors and set principles for external auditors providing nonaudit services.

Similarly, many other countries, including India, recommend that audit committees review and assess the external auditors' performance, make recommendations to the board for appointing or confirming the auditors, and approve nonaudit services.

Whatever requirements various countries may have, candid and ongoing communications between the external auditors and the audit committee are vital to an effective relationship. As is the case with the committee's relationships with management and internal audit, audit committee chairs interviewed point to the need to spend time with the external auditors between audit committee meetings.

Many audit committee chairs meet throughout the year with the external audit partner — usually quarterly but at least annually. Many chairs use these meetings to discuss the agenda of issues that will be covered at the upcoming meeting, as well as to understand any concerns on the partner's mind. The opportunity for candid conversation associated with such informal meetings allows for a free-form exchange of information. Chairs also use these sessions to corroborate their assessment of the quality of the external audit firm and the partner.

U.S. auditing standards proposed at the time of this publication (described further in Appendix C) would require external auditors to evaluate the two-way communications between the audit committee and the auditors as to whether the communication has been adequate to support issuing the audit opinion. Obviously, communications between the auditors and the audit committee should reflect a common interest in the reliability of the company's financial reporting.

2 | *Selection, reappointment, replacement, and evaluation of auditors*

One critical role for the audit committee is to select the audit firm and be comfortable with the assigned lead partner. To meet the company's needs, the audit firm must have the necessary resources on a variety of fronts — including industry experience, geographic reach, expertise in specialized areas of accounting, and ability to respond quickly to the company's requests.

Audit committees need to assess the auditors' performance before deciding to reappoint or replace them. Most committees use a variety of sources. Discussions with senior management and the internal audit director are helpful. Certainly, the audit committee members will have views on the external auditors' performance. And any audit committee members who serve on several audit committees, and thus have relationships with a number of audit firms, can draw on their experience to compare performance, confirm reputations, and identify issues.

Some external auditors engage the audit committee in specific discussions at the start of the year about performance expectations. Looking back on how the firm met those expectations is useful. Many audit firms also ask their senior or management partners who are not part of the audit engagement team to seek feedback from the audit committee (and from management) on how the firm is doing. The committee will wish to consider the firm's responsiveness in addressing any concerns raised in those discussions when assessing the firm's performance.

Exhibit 5.1 lists factors the committee should look for in selection, reappointment, or replacement decisions.

Exhibit 5.1	Factors in selecting, evaluating, reappointing, or replacing external auditors

- The firm's reputation

- The firm's knowledge and experience in the company's industry

- The lead partner's overall business acumen, knowledge and experience in the company's industry, and his or her personal credentials

- The engagement team's overall business acumen and knowledge and experience in the company's industry

- The scope of the external audit firm's international network and its ability to provide quality services across the company's international operations

- The lead partner's willingness to consult internally on issues and his or her ability to leverage other firm resources, as needed

- The committee's ability to build a trusting relationship with the lead partner, and his or her accessibility

- The lead partner's ability to clearly, candidly, and effectively communicate issues and concerns to the committee — both in private sessions and during meetings

- The engagement team's ability to work cooperatively with management — including the CEO and nonfinancial management — while maintaining objectivity

- The engagement team's ability to meet deadlines in providing services and to respond timely to issues

- The firm's quality control procedures

- Significant findings from recent firm inspections, peer reviews, or other governmental oversight reviews, if available

- The firm's independence and the systems it employs to ensure independence

In addition to forming their own viewpoint, audit committees should understand any shareholder concerns about the selection or reappointment of the external auditors. Although the audit committee has the responsibility to select external auditors, in many companies, shareholders vote on the selection. This ratification vote is neither binding nor required by law in the United States. However, if shareholders don't ratify the auditors' appointment, that sends a clear message to the audit committee as to shareholders' perception of the existing audit relationship.

An audit committee may decide to engage a new audit firm if the company is expanding to new territories or entering into highly complicated transactions that its current audit firm cannot adequately handle. In some cases, the audit committee will decide to change auditors if serious concerns arise over performance or independence that the audit firm cannot address.

Astute committees recognize that changing audit firms is disruptive and can be expensive. A newly appointed external audit firm must develop a deep understanding of the company, its accounting policies, internal controls, and the personalities of management and finance personnel. Plus, a change in audit firm requires management to spend more time and respond to an increased volume of requests, including for documentation that supports accounting positions that may have been in place for a number of years. Additionally, given the consolidation in the accounting profession and independence requirements, a company with an international presence and specific industry needs has few viable alternatives. Consequently, changes in audit firms are relatively infrequent.

Despite the challenges, the audit committee cannot ignore unresolved performance issues. One possible solution committees can consider if a performance problem arises is whether a different lead audit partner would resolve the issue.

If management recommends replacing the audit firm, the committee should satisfy itself that there are valid reasons and that the recommendation is not due to the auditors having a different perspective on accounting positions. In the United States, when a public company changes external auditors, management must file information about the change with the U.S. Securities and Exchange Commission (SEC), detailing any disagreements with the auditors. The auditors then submit a letter as to whether they agree with management's representations. The audit committee should understand whether the auditors have any disagreements to report.

Sometimes, audit firms choose to resign from a company's account. The committee should pay attention to any such resignation as a bellwether — potentially indicating elevated risks which could stem from changes in the business model, deteriorating control conditions, incompetent management, or poor reporting practices.

Some policy makers are proponents of rotating audit firms — changing firms periodically out of a belief that it promotes auditors' independence. Few countries, among them Italy and Brazil, have embraced mandatory rotation. That said, it is attracting more attention at the time of this publication, as European legislators explore auditor rotation as one possible way to improve financial reporting in light of the economic crisis.

Opponents of mandatory rotation policy believe that to be most effective, auditors need a deep understanding of the company and its business that often takes years to build. Indeed, the Committee of Sponsoring Organizations of the Treadway Commission (COSO) study, *Fraudulent Financial Reporting 1998–2007,* found that companies the SEC had charged with fraudulent financial reporting during that 10-year period were twice as likely to have changed auditors compared to a similar set of companies that did not have such fraud.

In most countries, the issue of auditors becoming too close to management, and thus compromising their independence, is addressed by changing audit partners periodically. While the decision as to which audit firm a company uses is of utmost importance, having the right individual serve as lead engagement partner is also vital. That individual plays a central role in harnessing audit firm resources to serve the company. The lead partner also needs to be able to work effectively with management.

It is not uncommon for the audit firm to bring more than one partner to meet and interview with management and audit committee members during a lead partner transition. This opportunity further enhances the committee's ability to make sure it has selected the right partner.

In many countries, including Australia and the United States, lead audit partners for public companies are limited to serving in that capacity for five consecutive years. The learning curve for a new lead partner is steep, as he or she needs to become familiar with the business and control environment and get to know financial reporting personnel and their capabilities. Given how steep the learning curve is, it is prudent for an incoming partner to "shadow" the outgoing partner for a period of time before assuming the lead partner role. This approach allows management and the audit committee to develop a more extensive relationship with the partner before he or she assumes the lead role.

At the end of the day, the audit committee needs to be comfortable with the diligence, capability, and professionalism of the lead partner. One audit committee chair interviewed indicated his belief that the committee has an "absolute obligation" to be comfortable the right person is leading the audit.

Interview insights
When we have a partner change coming up, I review the resumes. I also interview the candidates to judge whether they have the self-confidence to tell the audit committee what they think.
– AC Chair

Companies the SEC had charged with fraudulent financial reporting during that 10-year period were twice as likely to have changed auditors compared to a similar set of companies that did not have such fraud.

3 | *Auditor independence and objectivity*

Independence enables auditors to act with integrity and objectivity. Independence means they avoid any relationships with the company or management that might interfere with their ability to conduct the audit with an objective state of mind. For example, they would not be swayed by personal financial interests or joint business interests. And it is not only the fact of independence that is important — auditors must appear to be independent as well.

Audit committees take a direct role in confirming auditors' independence. In the United States, external auditors must, at least annually:

- Describe in writing to the audit committee all relationships between the audit firm and the company or managers in a financial oversight role that may reasonably be thought to bear on independence

- Discuss the potential effects of those relationships

- Affirm to the audit committee in writing that the audit firm is independent of the company

Regulatory and statutory rules in many other countries similarly require audit committees to assess external auditors' independence. In Australia, for example, audit committees fulfill this duty by using similar types of information. In the United Kingdom, the Combined Code on Corporate Governance states the audit committee should review and monitor the external auditors' independence and objectivity, taking into consideration U.K. professional and regulatory requirements.

Independence requirements for external auditors are both complicated and extensive. Partner rotation rules, as discussed above, are one aspect of the independence requirements. Other rules extend beyond the audit relationship. For example, if a company hires an individual in a financial reporting oversight role who, within a one-year period before the start of the company's audit, was on the audit engagement team, the external auditors would not be considered independent under SEC rules. For that reason, many audit committees have formalized policies for hiring staff members or partners from the external audit firm.

4 | *External audit scope*

External auditors are responsible for determining audit scope based on many factors, including their assessment of materiality (see Chapter 1) and risk. The audit committee should understand the external auditors' proposed scope and consider whether it is appropriate. And committees can ask auditors to perform additional work if, for example, specific areas of concern to the committee are not covered by internal audit's work.

Exhibit 5.2 lists some questions committees may wish to ask the external auditors about their audit scope and approach.

Exhibit 5.2	Illustrative questions about audit approach and scope

- What key risks have you identified and how does the audit plan address them?

- How will any recent changes in the company — such as mergers and acquisitions, restructurings, shifts in business strategy, changing product lines, modifications to pension plans, financing arrangements, or other unusual transactions — affect your audit approach?

- How did you define "materiality" in setting your scope?

- How are you gaining assurance over areas involving estimates?

- How are you identifying related party transactions?

- What extent of work do you plan to do on the company's information technology systems and applications?

- How will you coordinate your work with the internal auditors?

- What company locations will you visit this year? If you rotate visits to company locations, how do you determine which locations to visit and when?

- Which subsidiaries will you audit? What steps do you take for those not audited?

- If other audit firms are involved, will you assume responsibility for or refer to the work of the other auditors in your report? How do you as the principal auditor satisfy yourself that the work of the other auditors is acceptable and that they are independent?

For companies subject to external auditors' reporting on internal control, as described in Chapter 2, audit committees also need to consider the scope of that aspect of the auditors' work. Committees might ask such questions as: How are you evaluating the effectiveness of the company's internal control? What areas do you believe are at higher risk of having ineffective control? Are there any financial statement areas where you do not plan to rely on internal controls, and if not, why?

Audit committees should also understand any changes made to the audit plan — both as compared with the prior year and within the current year — and their implications. Changes in external audit scope may result from unusual and unforeseen transactions, mergers and acquisitions, and additional knowledge about a particular area. The audit committee should understand the reasons for any significant variances from the original audit plan. It also will want to understand the potential impact of scope revisions on audit fees.

5 | Audit fees

As well as preapproving all audit services, audit committees should understand both the proposed and final audit fees. In the United States, audit committees are responsible for overseeing the compensation for external auditors.

Auditors' fee estimates are based on the expected hours needed to complete the scope of work envisioned in the audit plan. Astute committees appreciate the importance of high-quality audits and recognize that audit fees need to reflect the thoroughness and level of service provided. Accordingly, committees don't necessarily seek lowest-cost audit services. Instead, they consider the fairness of audit fees in relation to the performance of a quality audit — taking into account the complexity of the company, the value the external audit firm provides, and the knowledge and expertise of the lead partner and audit team. But that does not mean committees are not concerned over fee levels.

How can committees ensure fee quotes are reasonable? In part, by relating them to the level of effort outlined in the audit plan. And by comparing them with what other companies of similar size and complexity are paying, which is relatively easy because companies in many countries disclose audit fees. Knowledgeable committees understand that many variables go into fee estimates, including levels of internal audit assistance, audit staff mix, complexity of the corporate structure, and whether separate audit opinions are required for certain subsidiaries. Benchmarking does, however, provide a basis for discussion among management, the auditors, and the audit committee about fees.

In most companies, management continues to play a key role in negotiating fees — assisting the audit committee with understanding the company's history of audit fees and providing insight before the audit committee's approval.

It is not unusual for the external auditors to incur cost overruns that exceed the original fee estimate from the audit planning stages. These overruns are sometimes attributable to changed facts and circumstances or unanticipated difficulties encountered in completing the audit. For example, an acquisition, merger, or restructuring can require changes to the initial audit plan. When budget overruns are incurred, auditors typically request additional fees for their unanticipated efforts. Committees should consider whether the extra hours stem from inefficiencies in the audit or poor planning. Conversely, overruns may result from unanticipated exceptions to audit test procedures or a lack of promised management assistance in the audit process. The audit committee needs to understand the factors contributing to the overrun before determining whether to approve such requests. Those factors also could point to problems with company personnel or controls.

6 | *Communication of audit results and insights*

Audit committees should discuss with the external auditors the progress of audit work throughout the year and the audit results once the audit is completed. Regulators and standard setters in many countries require certain information to be communicated to the audit committee — usually covering terms of the audit engagement, audit strategy and timing, and information about accounting policies and estimates. These communications can be either verbal or written but must be done before issuing the auditors' report. These communications can be made by either management or the auditors. Auditing standards require extensive, specific communications, which are outlined in Appendix C.

At times, audit committees may find it useful to discuss complex issues directly with the audit firm's specialized accounting, reporting, and auditing partners. These partners are often from the audit firm's "national office." By holding such discussions, the committee can better understand the audit firm's capabilities and gain insights from the experts involved in supporting the audit team.

While there are many required communications, external auditors also can provide other useful information to audit committees. The external audit team is in the unique position of having a deep understanding of the company's business, the capabilities of its finance team, its internal controls, the tone at the top, and the corporate culture, as well as influences on financial reporting personnel. The auditors also have experience working with other companies, thus they have the ability to benchmark the company's practices and share the knowledge accumulated from comparable audit experiences. Audit committees that embrace an open relationship with the external audit team may be more likely to benefit from such insights.

Interview insights
External auditors could add more value if they share more of their insights.
– AC Chair

7 | *Management representation letters*

External auditors request that management provide written representations on such matters as the collectibility of receivables, realizability of inventory, significant events that occurred after the balance sheet date, and knowledge of fraud and illegal acts. Management will also be asked to comment on other important matters such as whether reserves for specific matters are reasonable and whether specified intangible assets can be realized. Such letters confirm oral representations given to the external auditors, document the continued appropriateness of management's representations, and reduce the possibility of a misunderstanding.

Audit committees should review management representation letters. While the letter includes some standardized language, auditors often customize additional representations relating to highly judgmental accounting areas that may be unique to the individual company. The audit committee can gain further insight into the judgmental aspects of the company's accounting by asking the auditors to highlight those customized representations. The committee also might ask whether the auditors had any difficulties in obtaining any particular representation. Such difficulties could point to particularly sensitive areas requiring further committee attention.

8 | *Private sessions*

Interview insights
Private sessions are absolutely critical. I don't expect to hear information that contradicts what I heard in the meeting, but I do expect a clear point of view or clarification.

– AC Chair

It is customary for the audit committee to meet privately with the external auditors. Ideally, this should be done routinely, at each in-person audit committee meeting. These private sessions allow more open and candid discussion than might otherwise occur with management present and provide an opportunity for the committee to hear an objective point of view from the auditors. They also allow the audit committee to derive the maximum benefit from its relationship with the auditors.

The audit committee can prepare for these sessions by considering what questions to ask and not simply relying on whether the auditors volunteer any information.

Exhibit 5.3 includes examples of potentially insightful questions.

Exhibit 5.3	Possible questions for the private session with the external auditor

- Did you recommend any changes to the financial statements or press releases that were not made? If so, what were the areas and nature of the suggested changes?

- What areas of our financial reporting do you believe could be challenged or scrutinized by regulators?

- What do you believe is the quality of our reported earnings for the current period?

- What is your perception of the tone at the top and at the middle management level?

- How capable is our finance team?

- Do you believe that pressure is placed on individuals in the financial reporting group to achieve a desired outcome when addressing an accounting issue?

- Do you believe that management has appropriately dealt with individuals involved in fraudulent or questionable behavior?

- Does anything cause you concern about the way the company operates?

- What areas of the audit take the most time, are subject to budget overruns, or lead to recurring disagreements with management?

- What questions should we be asking of you and of management? Where should we be spending more time?

- How rehearsed and scripted are the presentations to the audit committee?

9 | Disagreements with external auditors

The audit committee should understand any disagreements between management and the external auditors. Given how challenging it is to account for complex transactions, those involved in financial reporting must devote more time and effort to ensure the accounting is appropriate. Management has to investigate, gather facts, and assess its position. External auditors evaluate and test the underlying information and assess the issues carefully. If disagreements between management and the auditors arise, audit committees can expect more involvement as well. Indeed, in the United States, audit committees have the responsibility to resolve significant disagreements regarding financial reporting.

Audit committees that find themselves involved in having to resolve disagreements should:

- Discuss the issue with management to understand the transaction and accounting implications, including alternative accounting treatments
- Discuss the issue with the external auditors to understand issues, concerns, and alternative and preferred accounting treatments

- Understand whether regulators have already expressed a view on the accounting issue
- Determine whether to consult additional resources
- Discuss resolution with management and external auditors

Audit committees tend to be reluctant to hire outside advisors to address the company's accounting issues. Instead, they usually look to resources within their external audit firms to assist them in forming a point of view. Larger accounting firms have many experts who specialize in various specific areas and deal with complex and emerging issues on a regular basis.

At the end of the day, the audit committee must be satisfied with the resolution of any significant disagreements. If the committee is not sufficiently comfortable, it should seek a second opinion from another accounting firm or consultant. Chairs of committees that have done so are quick to point out they were not "opinion shopping," but rather wanted to ensure they had all the information they needed to make an informed decision about the appropriateness of the accounting.

10 | Nonaudit services

Certain types and levels of nonaudit services and certain fee arrangements — such as contingency fees — may impair auditors' independence. Committees need to be aware of such factors when deciding to approve proposed nonaudit services. Indeed, U.S. rules require audit committees to preapprove nonaudit services.

In the United States, the SEC allows auditors to provide nonaudit services, as long as auditors do not:

- Audit their own work
- Make management decisions or function as management

- Serve in an advocacy role for the company
- Have a mutual or conflicting interest with the company

Using those principles, the SEC prohibits auditors from providing a few specific services, including legal services, executive recruiting, and investment banking.

In the first few years after Sarbanes-Oxley, many audit committees stopped using external auditors for nonaudit services. After a few years, however, committees became more comfortable having their external auditors perform allowable nonaudit services where it makes sense. Committees recognized it can be cost effective, given the external auditors have a deep understanding of the company, its personnel, and its business.

When determining whether the external auditors should be retained to perform allowable services, such as those outlined in Exhibit 5.4, audit committees might evaluate whether the auditors are the most competent service provider for the particular service, whether they have the skill sets, and whether having the audit firm provide the services may increase the audit firm's knowledge of the company, thus improving overall audit quality. Furthermore, in some cases, the external auditors will need to perform the same procedures as being done in the nonaudit services to support their audit opinion, thus duplicating effort and cost.

Exhibit 5.4	Generally permitted nonaudit services

Generally, external auditors may provide the following types of services for their audit clients without impairing their independence:

- Corporate tax return preparation
- Corporate tax planning and consulting
- Financial due diligence for acquisitions and post-merger integration

- Tax advice related to acquisitions and divestitures or new tax legislation
- Transfer pricing analysis
- Fraud and investigation analysis

Many countries — including Australia, Canada, India, the United States, and the United Kingdom — require companies to disclose fees paid to the auditors for audit and nonaudit services, by category. Shareholders and proxy advisory firms pay particular attention to the magnitude of nonaudit services that companies report. So, while many audit committees see benefit in using external auditors to perform certain nonaudit services, they also consider relative audit to nonaudit fee levels when making preapproval decisions.

11 | *Using other auditors*

There are times where management will use a different audit firm than the principal auditors. This can be driven by the need to seek additional accounting expertise or because it makes the most economic sense in the situation.

Occasionally, management may ask a second accounting firm for advice in connection with a complex technical accounting issue. This may be appropriate when the company is involved in matters where accounting standards are unsettled or the company does not have the deep technical resources to deal with the issue. The purpose of employing a second firm may be to confirm the advice of the company's external auditors or to gain additional insights into a position taken by another company in apparently similar circumstances.

Sometimes, a different audit firm is engaged to perform audits of some of the company's subsidiaries, equity investments, or employee benefit plans. Generally, there is a good reason — for example, when the principal auditors do not have an office convenient to a subsidiary location or a subsidiary was acquired recently and its former auditors are completing the audit in the acquisition year. Or, the company might be a party to a joint venture, and the auditors for the other investor(s) are auditing the joint venture.

Some companies with subsidiaries in many countries have separate audits performed of some of those subsidiaries — so-called "statutory audits" — as required by local authorities. The principal auditors may rely on certain work performed as part of those statutory audits in completing the consolidated audit. These separate audits can add significant costs to the company's overall external audit fees but are required. At times, a small, local audit firm may be involved in the smaller statutory audits. This is typically the case if those entities are not material to the company's consolidated results, if the principal auditors don't need to rely on any work performed for those statutory audits, and if the company is able to save costs by using a local audit firm.

The audit committee should be informed whether the company plans to use audit firms other than the principal auditors and should ensure the rationale for using such firms is appropriate. Audit committees also should understand whether the principal auditors are planning to assume responsibility for the work of the other auditors. In these situations, the committee should understand how the principal auditors assess the other firms' reputation, quality of staff, scope of work and results, and independence. Audit committees should consider whether they need to have direct involvement with the other firms — for example, by preapproving services and fees and receiving required communications.

6

What to Do When Things Go Wrong — Financial Statement Errors and Fraud Investigations

Audit committees sometimes have to address particularly difficult situations relating to financial reporting or compliance issues. Previously issued financial statements may be materially misstated. Fraud could possibly have occurred. Or the company may have violated laws or regulations.

Such situations bring challenges that few committee members are accustomed to dealing with. Further, each situation is unique and specific to the company's facts and circumstances, and each requires good decision-making that involves a great degree of judgment. One thing is clear: When things go wrong, it's not business as usual for the audit committee.

> *This chapter focuses on the following areas for audit committees to consider before things go awry:*
>
> 1. Errors in issued financial statements
> 2. Investigations involving possible fraud or illegal acts
> 3. Effective crisis management planning

1 | *Errors in issued financial statements*

The audit committee's central responsibility is overseeing the accuracy of financial reporting. Consequently, the audit committee needs to know if management becomes aware of a situation that suggests there may be an error in previously issued financial statements that is more than inconsequential.

If errors are identified, management must assess their materiality. If management, after consulting with the external auditors, concludes the impact of unintentional errors is inconsequential, it needs to document that conclusion contemporaneously, but doesn't need to take additional action. (Of course, if identified errors are intentional, they may constitute fraud and so the committee needs to consider an investigation, as outlined in the next section.) For more significant errors, management and the audit committee must determine whether the errors are material to the financial statements taken as a whole, and gain concurrence from the external auditors. If the effect of identified errors is concluded to be material, the company needs to restate. And the company must inform the public that the previously issued financial statements can no longer be relied on.

Not all restatements indicate a fraudulent act has occurred. Given the complexity of financial reporting standards, errors are sometimes attributable to mistakes in judgment or a lack of understanding. Regardless of whether the misstatement was intentional or the result of an error, any type of restatement can bring negative ramifications.

Restatements can drive a drop in the company's share price and can also raise questions among stakeholders about the integrity of the company's financial reporting processes and system of internal control. The investigation that's required to determine what accounts and amounts need to be restated can divert management's focus from running the business. Furthermore, the legal, external audit, and internal audit costs can be staggering.

Uncertainty also is created during the period between the date the company makes investors aware of a potential restatement and the date it provides the restated financial information. Though the decision on whether a restatement is needed may be made relatively quickly, in some cases, it can take years for a company to finalize corrected results.

Generally, a company does not file any financial reports with securities regulators until it understands the full impact of the identified errors. One implication of not being current on its filings is that the company is not allowed to raise new capital. So, the sooner corrected financial statements are available for investors' scrutiny, the faster management can refocus on running the business.

Discussions about possible restatements are even more difficult when executives' personal wealth is on the line. The 2010 Dodd-Frank Act requires U.S. public companies to adopt clawback policies to recoup incentive compensation paid to executives based on financial reports that subsequently were found to be erroneous. Audit committees should be aware of how such pressures may factor into management's judgments about the need for a restatement.

> *Interview insights*
> If the company is in trouble, we need to communicate more frequently. All committee members should be brought into those discussions and decisions.
> – AC Chair

The positive news is that, in the United States, the number of companies having to restate declined substantially between 2006 and 2010, from 1,566 companies to 699, according to Audit Analytics.

Larger companies have a significantly lower number of restatements than smaller companies, as Exhibit 6.1 shows. Larger companies tend to have more sophisticated systems of internal accounting control. Plus, the impact of an identified error may be less material to the financial results of a larger company than to a smaller one.

Exhibit 6.1	U.S. restatement demographics over a five-year period				
	2006	2007	2008	2009	2010
Larger U.S. companies	448	282	212	142	136
Smaller U.S. companies	887	630	472	385	424
Larger non-U.S. companies	39	37	17	14	12
Smaller non-U.S. companies	192	145	124	99	127
Total number of companies restating	1,566	1,094	825	640	699

Note: "Larger" companies are those with worldwide market capitalization of more than $75 million. Source: Audit Analytics. These represent restatements filed with the U.S. Securities and Exchange Commission (SEC).

Even when an identified problem was originally believed to be confined to one particular issue, it's not unusual that the company will identify additional potential accounting errors during an investigation. Also, as errors are identified and operating results are adjusted, the materiality threshold may change, which could require additional errors to be reflected in the restatement.

Audit committees will want to understand how management is ensuring the initial restatement corrects all errors. A thorough investigation can prevent a scenario where additional information becomes available after the original restatement is issued, and previously unidentified errors force another restatement. Such a situation would exacerbate the costs of restatement and further lessen confidence in the company's ability to accurately report results. That said, Audit Analytics found the U.S. average number of issues per restatement declined from 2.01 in 2006 to 1.48 in 2010.

Restatements often result in lawsuits. Plaintiffs usually claim they relied on the erroneous financial information. Many restatements cover extended reporting periods — a number of quarters or even years. Typically, the greater the period of restatement and the greater the dollar value of errors, the greater the company's exposure to litigation. Longer restatement periods also increase the number of people who claim they relied on the erroneous financial information. The good news is that, much like other U.S. restatement trends, Audit Analytics found the affected periods for which companies have to restate have been declining steadily — from 717 days in 2006 to 491 days in 2010, on average.

That said, even if companies ultimately aren't found liable in such lawsuits, the cost, distraction, and possible reputational damage are challenges directors need to address. Plus, shareholders and proxy advisory firms track directors of companies that restate, and so directors face possible personal reputational risk.

Certain areas within the financial statements have proven more vulnerable to restatement than others. Audit committees may want to look to these as areas of higher risk. Audit Analytics indicates the following areas were consistently more often subject to restatement between 2006–2010, although the number in each category fluctuated in these years.

- Debt, warrants, and equity

- Expense (payroll, selling, general and administrative) recording

- Liabilities, payables, reserves, and accrual estimates

- Deferred, stock-based, and/or executive compensation

- Revenue recognition

- Accounts and loans receivable, investments, and cash

- Statements of cash flows

- Acquisition, merger, disposal, and reorganization accounting

- Tax expenses

2 | *Investigations involving possible fraud or illegal acts*

Audit committees can guard against the occurrence of fraud and illegal acts by ensuring companies implement adequate compliance programs, as discussed in Chapter 2. The 2010 Association of Certified Fraud Examiners' *Report to the Nations on Occupational Fraud and Abuse* concluded that the implementation of antifraud controls (such as hotlines, employee support programs, and fraud training) showed a measurable reduction in fraud exposure.

However, sometimes information indicates that management or employees may have committed possible illegal or fraudulent acts. Both management and the audit committee need to handle such issues properly and prudently, as they can have a significant impact on the company's reputation and valuation. At times, fraudulent activity can even require companies to restate previously issued financial statements.

How does the audit committee know an investigation may be needed? Allegations of fraud or illegal acts may arise from a tip that came through the whistleblower hotline. Internal audit or the external auditors also may have identified some suspicious behavior through their work. The company may receive inquiries or notices from regulatory bodies that can spark the need for an investigation. Whatever the source, the key is that the committee — or the chair — have a process in place for being informed timely of significant matters. Furthermore, proactive committees have a protocol and an action plan ready to execute — since an allegation can come at any time.

Once informed, audit committee members should understand the substance and nature of the allegation to determine whether an investigation is needed. Audit committees may contact legal counsel, external auditors, or other experts to discuss the possible need for an investigation, as these individuals have significant knowledge and experience in dealing with such situations. The decision whether to investigate is based on the potential reach and magnitude of the issue or the committee's belief it is not getting appropriate answers to its questions.

Once the audit committee has determined that an investigation is needed, there are many elements to consider:

- ***Take action quickly.*** Investigations may have implications for ongoing financial reporting, capital- or debt-raising capabilities, and the magnitude of potential litigation. Quick action also helps ensure information that may be crucial is preserved.

- ***Decide on the investigation team.*** A preliminary assessment will help the committee decide whether to have independent third parties or internal resources conduct the investigation. Independent third parties should be selected if factors such as illegal acts, possibility of restatement, or potential senior management misbehavior exist.

- ***Determine who the investigation team will report to.*** Depending on the circumstances, executive management, the audit committee, or a special committee of independent directors may supervise the investigation team. If the issue under investigation relates to lower-level managers or external parties, it may be entirely appropriate for the team to report to management. But the audit committee or board will need to assume that responsibility if management is potentially part of the problem or is otherwise conflicted.

- ***Obtain the concurrence of relevant parties.*** External auditors will, and regulators possibly may, have to concur with the proposed scope of the investigation, the adequacy of the procedures, and the conclusion reached. Therefore, they need to be consulted on the investigation throughout the process so they can be confident the results are comprehensive and appropriate.

- ***Consider management.*** An investigation can be very disruptive and time-consuming. The executive team needs to focus on continuing to effectively lead the company, whether executives are involved in the investigation or not. The committee should monitor this issue.

- ***Obtain the right counsel.*** The involvement of legal counsel (in-house or outside) is crucial, as lawyers are in the best position to determine whether an act requires investigation and how to proceed. When hiring external counsel, companies should focus on the firm's experience with the matters under investigation. It's important legal counsel be independent if the investigation involves allegations against management. Another consideration is the lawyers' credibility with any outside parties or regulators that may rely on the investigation.

- ***Use the right advisors and resources.*** Companies will also need access to other experts or advisors to assist with the investigation — for example, forensic accountants, experts on complex accounting transactions, specially trained investigators, or internal audit staff. Typically, legal counsel will engage these other advisors so their work is done under privilege.

- ***Consider notifying investors and regulators.*** In the United States, the SEC has articulated a framework for evaluating a company's response to issues, which it uses in determining what enforcement action to take. One factor in the framework is whether a company conducts a thorough investigation of the nature, extent, origins, and consequences of potential misconduct. Another key is whether the company also self-reports promptly and completely — disclosing that misconduct to the public and regulators. It may also be important to cooperate with law enforcement authorities, providing relevant information about the violations and the company's remediation efforts.

- *Meet documentation requirements.* Companies have to ensure they preserve underlying records, even if they may contain incriminating information. They also need to be able to demonstrate how the investigation was conducted and what underlying information was examined. Legal counsel will advise on which documentation — including emails and records of phone calls — must be preserved once an investigation is launched.

- *Manage communications.* Company personnel need to understand the importance of the investigation and provide their full cooperation. Personnel may need to retain documentation as instructed. Careful consideration should be given to what is reported externally. Questions should be handled by a single, competent spokesperson.

- *Monitor progress.* The audit committee needs to be kept apprised of progress. It should concur on the need to expand or limit the investigation as more facts become known and to engage additional resources.

Once the investigation is complete, the audit committee should review key findings and discuss appropriate responses. What steps, including improvements to internal control, are needed to reduce the likelihood of recurrence? Were wrongdoers dismissed or appropriately disciplined? What has the company learned that could make any future investigations run more smoothly?

Audit committees that have experience with overseeing investigations know to keep vigilant for common pitfalls, as described in Exhibit 6.2.

Exhibit 6.2	Common pitfalls when conducting investigations

- Presuming that an internal process will satisfy all parties and regulators relying on the investigation, and so not engaging external advisors

- Hiring outside experts and counsel to conduct the investigation who lack the requisite experience and credibility or are not independent

- Not obtaining the initial concurrence of regulators and external auditors on the scope of the investigation; then having difficulty convincing those parties to rely on the investigation's results

- Having an inadequate investigation, thereby exposing the company to further scrutiny about its credibility

- Not retaining sufficient documentation of the procedures performed and so being unable to adequately defend the results of the investigation

- Rushing through the process, since an investigation that is not thorough won't satisfy all parties relying on the work

- Allowing management to become over-absorbed in the investigation and to lose focus on running the business

- Losing objectivity when dealing with management and not taking action when the findings suggest that punitive action should be taken

In some countries, such as Australia and the United States, both the external auditors and the audit committee have statutory responsibility to investigate possible illegal acts. If management and the board don't take timely and appropriate remedial action with respect to an allegation of an illegal act, external auditors in the United States are required to report the matter to the SEC.

3 | Effective crisis management planning

Companies rarely know when they'll have to manage a crisis. Being prepared can provide considerable benefits for managing a crisis if one does occur. In many cases, the full board will directly oversee the response to operational or environmental crises. However, the audit committee typically oversees many other crises — particularly those relating to financial reporting, illegal acts, or certain aspects of compliance.

Some directors don't know whether their companies have a crisis management plan prepared. The PwC *2010 Annual Corporate Directors Survey* indicates that only two-thirds of responding directors had discussed an action plan during the prior year that would outline the steps the company would take if facing a major crisis.

Crises happen even when a company has followed preventative measures. A crisis management plan can help the company respond to a crisis when real-time decision-making is critical.

Audit committees should discuss whether management has a comprehensive crisis management plan in place. That plan will help the company respond effectively if a problem arises. Although the exact nature of many crises cannot be predicted, the plan should outline protocols, procedures, and key decisions, including whether an investigation is needed, whether management should be involved, and such other factors as discussed earlier in this chapter. The plan also should identify key information (perhaps including contracts, insurance policies, etc.) and contact details for company personnel who need to be involved and potential outside advisors that the company likely will engage.

For more information about the board's role in handling a crisis, see *Board Effectiveness — What Works Best,* 2nd edition.

Discussions about possible restatements are even more difficult when executives' personal wealth is on the line.

7

Committee Composition

An audit committee's effectiveness depends greatly on the composition and interaction of its membership. Selecting appropriate members is essential. Combining new members who can introduce valuable insights on the committee's processes with experienced members who bring institutional knowledge can result in a highly effective team.

This chapter discusses the following key considerations for committee composition:

1. Selecting committee members

2. The committee chair

3. Members' attributes

   i. Financial knowledge

  ii. Independence

4. Committee size

1 | *Selecting committee members*

One factor to keep in mind when considering committee composition is how long members have served. Boards need to balance the benefits of having experienced members oversee complex financial reporting against the risk that, after serving on the committee for a number of years, some members may become complacent. To address this issue, some boards have informal term limits, often ranging from five to seven years. Others believe the normal turnover of directors solves this problem.

The Society of Corporate Secretaries & Governance Professionals' *Current Board Practices, Sixth Study* indicates that fewer than one in five boards have a policy to rotate committee membership, although it is more common at larger companies. Boards that rotate directors — either formally or informally — stagger the terms of service for committee members to help ensure new members have the benefit of guidance from more experienced members.

When the company doesn't have a policy to change committee composition, regular evaluation of individual committee members' performance becomes more important. Evaluations help ensure members are contributing as expected.

Even without a rotation policy, new audit committee members are periodically needed to replace departing members, add a needed skill set, or expand the committee size temporarily. Astute chairs avoid the situation of adding many new members within a short period, understanding the benefit of having a core of experienced members who can provide continuity and perspective. Therefore, if the chair knows that within a few years a number of members will be exiting — for example, if they are approaching the board's mandatory retirement age — it can be wise to temporarily expand the committee's size so new members have an adjustment period before the experienced members depart.

Who decides which directors to place on the committee? Leading practice would have the nominating/governance committee oversee appointing audit committee members. Since the nominating/governance committee is responsible for the selection of directors and the effectiveness of the entire board and its committees, it should be well positioned to understand individual directors' strengths and ensure the committee has the right composition. The *Current Board Practices, Sixth Study* found that the nominating committee had primary responsibility for appointing committee members (and chairs) at half the public companies covered in the survey.

Many observers believe the CEO should have limited involvement in selecting the committee members or chair, given the committee's key role in overseeing management's judgments. But as a board member, the CEO will have a view on prospective committee members.

> *Interview insights*
> Former CEOs and CFOs are good to have on the committee — they have a pragmatic approach.
> – AC Chair

> *Interview insights*
> We require a high level of engagement from our audit committee members.
> – AC Chair

The audit committee chair has important insight into skill sets that a new member ideally would bring to supplement the committee's strengths. The chair understands whether additional expertise on the committee would better help it oversee the company's complex transactions. An astute chair also understands that assembling a committee that includes members with nonfinancial backgrounds can improve the dialogue, as those members add value by bringing different perspectives when the committee is reviewing financial reports.

At times, no other current board directors will have the skill set that the audit committee seeks. Consequently, the board has to decide whether to recruit a new director.

Should a new board member be immediately appointed to the audit committee? One benefit is that the scope of audit committee oversight provides an excellent opportunity for a new director to learn about the company. Conversely, a new director would have to learn about the company, the industry, and the company's financial reporting processes at the same time — which could entail a steep learning curve. And given that antitrust provisions in some countries make it difficult to recruit directors with in-depth industry knowledge — plus the practical matter that companies want to avoid having competitors on their boards — any new directors need a good orientation program.

2 | *The committee chair*

An audit committee's effectiveness depends greatly on the chair's skills and dedication. The person must have the time and energy for the role and should understand the major financial reporting issues to direct the committee's focus on properly addressing high-risk areas.

Those criteria are evident in the profile of current chairs. Many audit committee chairs are retired, giving them the time to fulfill the role. Indeed, Spencer Stuart's *2010 Board Index* finds the most prevalent background for audit committee chairs is retired executives — board chairs, CEOs, and presidents — at 27%. The second most prevalent background for chairs, at 20%, represents the deep financial expertise that a CFO, treasurer, or financial manager brings. Active board chairs, CEOs, and presidents chair committees at only 13% of the large companies covered in the *2010 Board Index*, while those identified as "accountants" chair 10% of the audit committees.

The chair also needs strong leadership and facilitation skills and the ability to promote effective working relationships — among committee members, management, and internal and external auditors. The most effective chairs also develop a sense of whether there is any underlying concern that isn't surfacing in the meeting discussion and draw it out, either in executive session or offline.

Similar to committee membership overall, it's good practice for the nominating/governance committee to take primary responsibility for selecting the chair. However, smaller companies may be more inclined to use the full board to make that selection.

Another important consideration is planning for succession of the chair role, and a thoughtful process can ease the transition. A new chair is better prepared to lead the committee if he or she has experience working with the other committee members. Ideally, once the successor chair is identified, that individual can join the committee (if not already a member) and spend time "shadowing" and learning from the activities of the outgoing chair before assuming the leadership role. Of course, since audit committee members understand how considerable the time commitment is for chairs, some may be reluctant to take on the role.

Anecdotal evidence suggests that audit committee chairs of large companies spend approximately 50 to 100 additional hours annually fulfilling their chair duties.

3 | Members' attributes

Audit committee members must dedicate substantial time and energy to their role. They need to review financial reports (which can be voluminous), review information covering the many other responsibilities the committee has, travel to and attend meetings, and be prepared to devote even more time if a problem arises. Committee members also should commit to educational sessions about accounting, regulatory, and industry developments.

Financial knowledge and independence are particularly significant attributes for committee members, and are discussed in more detail below. *Other relevant attributes include:*

- Extremely high level of integrity
- Healthy skepticism
- Inquisitiveness and independent judgment — asking the right questions and appropriately interpreting the answers

- Courage to challenge answers that don't appear right
- Knowledge of the company's risks and controls
- Ability to offer new perspectives and constructive suggestions

> *Interview insights*
> Being a director on more than one company helps. You can compare materials received from different companies, taking away what's most valuable from each.
> – AC Chair

Recognizing the significant workload entailed in audit committee service, many companies establish policies limiting the number of audit committees on which a director can serve. Indeed, the New York Stock Exchange (NYSE) rules require a director who serves on more than three public company audit committees to get approval in each case from the board of directors.

The Spencer Stuart *2010 Board Index* reports that 41% of U.S. companies limit the number of audit committees a director can serve on, with most setting the limit at two. The National Association of Corporate Directors' *2010 Public Company Governance Survey* reports 50% of companies have a policy to limit the number of public company audit committees.

i. Financial knowledge

Having a robust understanding of financial reporting and the audit function is vital. Requirements around the world reflect the importance of this understanding.

In the United States, both the NYSE and the National Association of Securities Dealers rules require that all audit committee members be "financially literate" — able to understand fundamental financial statements. In India, similarly, all audit committee members are to be financially literate with at least one having accounting or related financial management expertise. The United Kingdom's Combined Code on Corporate Governance requires that at least one audit committee member have recent and relevant financial experience.

The Australian Stock Exchange Corporate Governance Council encourages publicly listed companies to have at least one audit committee member with financial expertise. In Canada, public companies must disclose the education and financial experience of all audit committee members. And in the Netherlands, at least one audit committee member must be a financial expert, defined in the Corporate Governance Code as someone with relevant knowledge and experience of financial administration and accounting for listed companies or other large legal entities.

The U.S. Securities and Exchange Commission (SEC) requires companies to disclose whether the audit committee has at least one member who qualifies as an "audit committee financial expert," as defined in the SEC's rules. *To meet this definition a member must have all of the following attributes:*

- An understanding of generally accepted accounting principles and financial statements
- The ability to assess the general application of such principles in connection with the accounting for estimates, accruals, and reserves
- Experience preparing, auditing, analyzing, or evaluating financial statements that present a breadth and level of complexity of accounting issues that are generally comparable to the breadth and complexity of issues that can reasonably be expected to be raised by the company's financial statements, or experience actively supervising one or more persons engaged in such activities
- An understanding of internal controls and procedures for financial reporting
- An understanding of audit committee functions

Some audit committees have multiple members meeting the "financial expert" definition. The Conference Board's *2010 U.S. Directors' Compensation and Board Practices Report* indicates that 53% of companies have a majority or all members of their audit committees who qualify as financial experts.

It's important that all committee members be engaged. The "nonexpert" members need to recognize the value their different perspectives contribute to the committee and be willing to ask about items they don't understand.

Regardless of applicable rules, audit committees need members with sufficient knowledge of accounting and financial reporting to enable them to understand the financial reporting process, financial statements, and related business issues. With the increasing complexity of business transactions and accounting and reporting principles and practices, members need to be positioned to ask the right questions and probe as necessary. Candid assessments of members' financial knowledge can help in determining where supplementary training and instruction may be useful.

ii. Independence

In its role overseeing the financial reporting process and representing the interests of shareholders, an audit committee often must question management's judgment or challenge its position. Consequently, independence is essential. Indeed, a committee composed only of independent directors is a leading practice — and in many countries is a requirement.

In the United States, for example, all audit committee members must be independent, with limited exceptions for newly public companies. The Combined Code on Corporate Governance in the United Kingdom requires audit committee membership to be confined to independent, nonexecutive directors. In Canada, the Ontario Securities Commission proposes that audit committees have only independent directors. While Australia encourages completely independent audit committees, its minimum requirement is for a majority of the members to be independent. The Dutch Corporate Code allows one member of the audit committee to be nonindependent. The Indian requirements call for two-thirds of the audit committee to be independent.

Who defines "independence"? Regulators, stock exchanges, and other organizations have developed rules or definitions that can guide companies in setting the committee's independence guidelines. The specific rules in various countries are readily available, and a director with a question about the requirements can consult the rules.

It is important to recognize, however, that a director who technically complies with the independence rules still might not be independent if other factors prevent that director from exercising true objectivity. The ultimate goal is member independence and objectivity in mind, action, appearance, and fact. Rules and guidelines set the minimum standard.

4 | *Committee size*

What is the optimal committee size? U.S. stock exchanges require audit committees to have at least three members. Canadian, Australian, and Indian public company audit committees also must have at least three members. The U.K. Combined Code on Corporate Governance has the same requirement for publicly listed companies, but allows smaller companies to have as few as two members.

If there is a minimum, is there an upper limit? Having more than three members provides a broader experience base, which can be valuable given the broad scope of a committee's mandate. However, large committees may be unwieldy and lose focus in meetings. They also may reduce the responsibility individual members feel, as one member might presume another will address a troubling issue.

Audit committees of three to six members are common. This range allows for active participation of members while keeping the size manageable. The Conference Board's *2010 U.S. Directors' Compensation and Board Practices Report* indicates the median size of an audit committee is four members. That size appears consistent across a number of countries. For example, a *Corporate Governance Assessment Summary Report on the Top 100 Chinese Listed Companies for 2009* shows an average audit committee size of 3.7. Spencer Stuart's *2010 Spain Board Index* reports companies have an average of four committee members. Ultimately, the committee's size should be determined by the company's circumstances.

8

Meetings

The most productive meetings are those in which the committee engages in relevant, candid, and interactive discussion with management and the auditors, as well as among its own members. Audit committees have many complex responsibilities to discharge, so it's not surprising they usually meet more frequently and for longer than the other two key board committees — compensation and nominating/governance. While phone meetings and other offline communications are increasingly important, the face-to-face meeting remains the key venue for the committee to discharge its responsibilities. As such, it must be well planned, coordinated, and executed to maximize committee effectiveness.

This chapter outlines the key attributes for successful audit committee meetings as follows:

1. Schedule
2. Frequency and duration
3. Agenda
4. Briefing materials
5. Participants
6. Private sessions
7. The chair's role
8. Meeting dynamics
9. Minutes
10. Reporting to the board

1 | *Schedule*

Audit committees need to determine when to meet throughout the year. Companies often schedule committee meeting dates a year or two in advance so members can plan their calendars.

Having an advance calendar helps a committee ensure it addresses all its responsibilities over the course of a year. Such a calendar lists the committee's responsibilities down one side and the expected meeting dates across the top, and it indicates how the responsibilities are allocated across meetings. While timing requirements drive some allocations (e.g., dates when key corporate reports are filed with securities regulators), other duties can be assigned over the course of the year to balance the work across meetings. Additionally, other expected activities — such as educational sessions — can be incorporated into the advance schedule.

An example of a scheduling calendar excerpt is shown in Exhibit 8.1. Such a tool also serves as the basis for drafting agendas of individual meetings.

Exhibit 8.1	**Excerpt from a sample audit committee schedule planner**

(December 31 year end)

Fundamental responsibilities from the audit committee charter	January 30 (phone)	February 15	March 1	April 30 (phone)	May 11 (phone)	June 1	July 31 (phone)	August 10 (phone)	September 20	October 31 (phone)	November 10 (phone)
Discuss the draft earnings releases	●			●			●			●	
Review the interim financial statements before filing					●			●			●
Review the annual audited financial statements and annual report			●								
Discuss with management and the external auditors any significant financial reporting issues and significant judgments	●			●			●			●	
Review internal audit risk assessment, plans, and resources			●			●					
Review significant findings from internal audit work		●				●			●		
⋮											

2 | *Frequency and duration*

How frequent and long should audit committee meetings be? Audit committees generally hold four or five in-person meetings and an additional four to eight telephonic meetings each year. Many audit committees add special meetings to address crises or to allow a venue for educational discussions.

The telephonic meetings typically are brief (less than an hour) and focus on the earnings press release, interim financial statements, and related data. They are generally held immediately before the date of the earnings release or the interim financial statement filing.

The in-person meetings are longer and accommodate in-depth discussions. These provide an opportunity for the committee to drill down into more complex areas and interact with management and the auditors.

The Spencer Stuart *2010 Board Index* indicates audit committees hold on average 8.8 meetings a year. At almost half of the companies, the audit committees convened eight to 10 times a year. At one-quarter of the companies, the audit committees met more than 11 times per year.

Too many variables exist to establish a standard or minimum meeting length. Rather, the committee should have enough time to cover the agenda effectively. The acid test is whether committee members are satisfied they have properly addressed significant agenda items, without undue pressure to rush discussions.

The PwC *2010 Annual Corporate Directors Survey* found in-person audit committee meetings last between two and four hours at 66% of companies; at 16% of companies, they run even longer.

It is vital that committee members have sufficient time to discuss important matters. While committee meetings often are scheduled to coincide with board meetings, they should not be so tightly scheduled as to restrict time needed to fully discuss issues. There should be flexibility to extend discussion if needed.

On the other hand, longer meetings are not necessarily better. Why? Because it is difficult to remain focused for extended periods. That is why, increasingly, committee chairs are shifting focus to ensuring efficient meetings. They expect that committee members have reviewed advance materials, then limit formal presentations during meetings so members can spend meeting time actively discussing issues, instead of passively listening.

3 | *Agenda*

Audit committee members should receive a detailed written agenda, along with briefing materials, well in advance of each meeting. Agendas help the committee focus on accomplishing what it needs to do. As mentioned earlier, a scheduling calendar can be used as a starting point in developing the agenda for each meeting.

Management usually drafts the meeting agenda for the committee chair. Most often, this responsibility falls to the internal audit director, the corporate secretary, or someone on the finance team — either the CFO or the controller. Some chairs participate in an agenda planning call with management and the auditors to identify possible topics. The chair should play an active role in ensuring all relevant issues are included and shape the agenda to his or her satisfaction before it is distributed.

It's common for chairs to invite other committee members to suggest agenda topics. Some chairs more actively involve other committee members by having the draft agenda for the next meeting included in the materials for the current meeting. This technique drives specific meeting discussion about topics to cover in the future.

Some committees use agendas that include the meeting time expected to be devoted to each topic. Timed agendas have certain advantages. They give management and the auditors an idea of how long a discussion to prepare for. Timed agendas also allow the chair to monitor progress during the meeting. Of course, astute chairs aren't bound by the suggested timing and insist on whatever time is needed to discuss complex issues. And if some topics run long, the chair can decide to postpone an item to another meeting.

Agendas are most useful in helping committee members prepare for the meeting when they clearly indicate how the agenda links to the briefing materials and what is being asked of the committee. Is the report being provided to the committee to obtain its advice? To get its approval? Or for informational purposes?

4 | Briefing materials

To enhance effectiveness, audit committee members should receive briefing materials ideally at least one week before meetings. For their part, committee members must take the necessary time to prepare fully by studying the materials provided.

Generally, materials are prepared and distributed by management and often include reports from the CFO or controller, the internal audit director, and external auditors. Some companies provide additional information to committee members between meetings, better enabling members to stay on top of issues and trends developing at the companies and providing them a more robust understanding of the results.

The best briefing materials strike the right balance — communicating the information the committee needs, yet avoiding extraneous detail. Leading practice is to have an executive summary at the start of each report in the briefing package. Writing this summary requires management or the auditors to analyze what they are communicating and think carefully about what is most important to the audit committee. An executive summary should provide context and allow committee members to grasp the important "bottom-line" messages in the report. The remainder of the report then provides expanded insight.

Many committees receive briefing packages that contain reports in the form of a presentation. Some of these presentations contain only a few words per bullet and are really meant for the meeting discussion. Committees should feel empowered to request that management either drop those reports or expand them so the committee can derive useful information.

Over the past decade many audit committees have been receiving increasingly detailed reports, giving members the opportunity to review the information that underlies certain key decisions. In some cases, this level of detail is at the request of regulators. But this trend concerns both audit committee chairs and governance observers. Many committees feel buried under the volume of information they are receiving. The sheer amount of detail makes it a challenge to discern what the issues are and whether the audit committee should be concerned about a particular area. As one observer who frequently interacts with audit committees put it, "Paper doesn't inform the audit committee."

Astute chairs recognize that it's difficult for management and internal audit to remove or condense reports that have always been part of the reporting package. And so those chairs are challenging management to reconsider the level of detail or how it's provided; they are suggesting instead that management consider other techniques, such as exception reporting in some areas or better use of graphics.

Audit committee members are all too aware of how voluminous their materials are — especially when a briefing package contains drafts of annual reports with full narrative reporting. This is a particular burden for directors who travel widely, as management must ensure the package gets to the right address.

Management teams have been leveraging technology to ease the physical burden. In PwC's *2010 Annual Corporate Directors Survey,* 46% of directors indicate their board has a secure Internet location where they can access sensitive board documents — up from 28% in 2006. Technology use will likely increase further as more companies adopt tablet technology to distribute audit committee (and board) materials. Management should be able to explain how it is securing any information it sends outside the company's systems.

5 | *Participants*

The chief financial officer, controller, internal audit director, external auditors, and corporate secretary typically attend every audit committee meeting. Because management is responsible for the financial reporting process, its active participation in committee meetings is important. The CEO and general counsel may also attend meetings. Functional specialists or business managers such as the compliance officer, chief risk officer, chief information officer, tax director, treasurer, chief operating officer, or business unit leaders also may attend certain meetings — typically when their expertise is needed to address a specific agenda item. Experienced chairs point to the need for CEOs to be "on call" during meetings if they are not attending in person.

To maximize effectiveness and support an atmosphere that allows frank discussion of sensitive matters, the committee should limit attendance to those who can make a contribution to agenda topics. Experience shows that a small group does better at getting to the heart of issues and dealing with them effectively.

An advantage to having several members of management attend is that the committee can get all of its questions answered during the meeting. However, there are drawbacks. When management and observers greatly outnumber the audit committee, members may be reluctant to ask questions. Also, a manager may be less candid in answering a question when his or her supervisor or peers are in attendance. Thus, while management can provide information helpful to the committee in its deliberations, the committee must remain alert so that management does not, unintentionally or otherwise, divert attention from sensitive matters.

Few audit committees routinely invite outside parties to meetings, except for the external auditors. But sometimes the committee needs to hear from other specialists, such as environmental engineers, pension or actuarial consultants, or lawyers who are conducting a special investigation at the committee's request.

Other directors usually are allowed to attend committee meetings, if they choose. Indeed, some boards avoid scheduling other board committee meetings concurrently for this reason. And a trend at some companies is for many of the other directors to attend audit committee meetings. Where that is not common practice, the board may suggest that new board members attend audit committee meetings because the discussion provides valuable insight on the company's business, risks, and operations.

6 | *Private sessions*

The audit committee should meet regularly in separate private (or executive) sessions with the internal audit director, the external auditors, and management. Private sessions allow either the committee or the other party to discuss more sensitive issues or topics they weren't comfortable raising in an open meeting. Such sessions also provide an opportunity to discuss auditors' performance, management's performance, and how the committee might improve its own performance. Many committees hold private sessions at each face-to-face meeting. These private sessions should be scheduled as part of the agenda, and chairs should ensure they actually are held.

Indeed, the New York Stock Exchange rules require audit committees to hold regular private sessions with internal audit, the external auditors, and management.

Committees may find it useful to have additional periodic private sessions with other parties — general counsel, the CEO, the chief compliance officer, or the chief risk officer. Meeting privately, at least annually, with managers from these functions is particularly important if the audit committee oversees their work as part of its responsibility or if these parties are a source of information that impacts the financial statements.

Finally, audit committees should also hold member-only sessions to have time to discuss their concerns and performance. The chair will take the lead in communicating any requests from these sessions back to management.

7 | The chair's role

Committee chairs play a crucial role in ensuring that meetings function effectively. But their role starts well before a meeting. Many chairs hold one or more premeetings with the internal audit director, external auditors, and key finance management a week or two before the committee meeting. These discussions allow the chair to better understand developments, issues, and the status of prior issues. Some chairs also review the briefing materials before they are sent to the full committee, ensuring the materials best serve the committee's needs.

The chair takes the lead in any follow-up after the meeting by communicating requests from private sessions or discussing how management will resolve any open items. The chair also engages in conversations between meetings, tracking how the open items are being addressed.

> *Interview insights*
> Premeetings with auditors help alert me to areas to emphasize in meetings.
> – AC Chair

8 | Meeting dynamics

In discussing meeting frequency, length, agendas, advance materials, and participants, it's easy to lose sight of how the meetings run. The meetings have to facilitate meaningful discussion by the committee. And they should avoid being heavily scripted or overly formal.

Part of the dynamics supporting effective meetings is to ensure — to the extent possible — that there are no surprises. If management knows about a major concern ahead of time, the chair should be told. If the chair or other members have particular concerns, they should tell management before the meeting that they would like an issue addressed. Indeed, some committees send their questions on the material to management before the meeting so management can better prepare. That does not mean no new questions will arise during meetings. But avoiding surprises where possible ultimately leads to more productive meetings and builds an atmosphere of mutual respect.

Another technique chairs use is to remind a presenter that the committee has read the materials and the presenter doesn't have to repeat what is in them. Instead, the presenter can set context and hit the high points, and then the committee can quickly move to discussion. Similarly, if the company commonly provides multipage presentations in advance materials, the chair may limit the number of slides that the manager can present in the meeting.

> *Interview insights*
> Chairs need to encourage committee members to question, challenge, and speak out during meetings. This is important as people from this part of the world are nonconfrontational.
> – AC Chair

Certain presenters may be ineffective when presenting at committee meetings, and the chair may need to direct senior management to counsel an individual on the most appropriate way to deliver information. If that person cannot improve with coaching, the chair should direct management to have a different person cover that topic with the committee.

Another approach that more chairs are embracing is the use of a "consent agenda." Under this approach, if there are no questions, the committee doesn't have to discuss routine topics at all. This allows the committee to focus on the more important topics.

Experienced chairs also know how to keep meetings from devolving into editing sessions. They ensure there is a channel or mechanism for committee members to communicate directly to the finance team with their less-critical, grammatical, or editorial comments on draft financial statements.

Chairs often face a delicate challenge when running meetings. They have to allow for proper discussion of topics and respect all committee members' concerns, but not allow the conversation to stray far into areas that aren't central to the issue under discussion. Some chairs are particularly effective at allowing a discussion to proceed for a period, then bringing the committee's focus back to the agenda by suggesting the remainder of the discussion be taken offline. This requires skill, though. If chairs cut off conversation too quickly, they can create an atmosphere that reduces dialogue.

Although much falls on the chair, all committee members bear collective responsibility for the effectiveness of meetings and should discuss any suggestions for improvement.

9 | *Minutes*

The company needs to keep a record of committee meetings, so minutes are important. Combined with agendas and briefing packages, minutes document how the committee discharges its assigned responsibilities.

One central question is how much detail should the minutes reflect? They should reflect the topics covered, the total time the committee spent in the meeting, who attended, and the conclusions reached. Ideally, minutes will demonstrate the process the committee used to discuss or resolve issues, the individuals who participated in such discussions, the relevant information the committee considered, and that it acted independently of management when reaching its conclusion. Minutes should also provide enough information for members to draw on if questions arise years later as to what the committee did or what it considered in a certain situation. For these reasons, many committees have shifted to minutes that provide insight into the topics discussed, moving away from bare bones minutes. That said, they avoid having minutes resembling transcripts — with details on which member asked which question.

Audit committees need to pay attention to minutes. Astute directors recognize that minute taking is an art, not an administrative function. The secretary for the committee needs to exercise judgment in recording minutes that reflect the right level of detail. For that reason, committees often ask company lawyers to draft the minutes, as those individuals understand the implications of how details are captured. Committees also carefully review draft minutes; before granting approval, they can require changes if they are uncomfortable with what has been captured or the way it has been represented.

Committees need to ensure that follow-up actions identified during the meeting are addressed. Some choose to have a section of the minutes capture those items. Others rely on management to note and track the follow-up needed.

Minutes of private sessions typically are not recorded. But the minutes should indicate which private sessions were held.

10 | *Reporting to the board*

The audit committee needs to report regularly to the board so other directors understand how it discharged its responsibilities and what issues it addressed. The audit committee chair briefs the board on issues and decisions following each meeting.

The chair typically uses his or her discretion in determining what information and at what level of detail to report. A chair might also use the private session with fellow audit committee members to review the key issues they believe should be reported and reach consensus. If most of the other directors attend the audit committee meeting, the chair can be more concise when reporting to the board.

Copies of approved minutes from audit committee meetings are also usually provided to the board.

9

Supporting Committee Effectiveness — Charter, Evaluations, Resources, and Training

A written audit committee charter helps ensure that committee members — as well as other board directors — understand which roles are assigned to the audit committee. An evaluation process is critical for monitoring the committee's performance and identifying opportunities for improvement. Some of those opportunities may involve educational sessions that help the committee understand new developments and how they impact the company. Committees also need to be able to leverage resources to support them in carrying out their responsibilities.

This chapter focuses on these processes that support the committee's effectiveness:

1. Charter
2. Committee evaluations
    i. Individual member assessment
    ii. Frequency of assessment
3. Resources
4. Training and education
    i. New member orientation
    ii. Ongoing development

1 | *Charter*

A written charter should document the audit committee's duties in a manner that clearly communicates the committee's scope. A charter assists with agenda setting for committee meetings and provides checkpoints for the committee, allowing it to track activities. The charter also helps communicate to stakeholders exactly what the committee does. Exhibit 9.1 outlines the areas a charter typically covers.

Exhibit 9.1	Typical charter items

- Purpose/mission
- Size and member attributes (e.g., independence, financial knowledge)
- Meeting frequency and private sessions
- Roles and oversight responsibilities
- Reporting responsibilities
- Authority

The charter should comply with the company's listing and regulatory requirements while providing the audit committee with the flexibility to take on additional responsibilities, as needed. An astute audit committee also knows to ensure its charter isn't too specific — for example, specifying when the committee handles a responsibility or mandating that certain discussions happen at every meeting — because such language increases noncompliance risk.

Written charters are a requirement for many public companies. In the United States, audit committees of public companies have to adopt written charters, include these charters in their proxy statements periodically, and post them on their websites. Other countries, such as the United Kingdom and Australia, have similar requirements.

It's a good idea to review the charter periodically to ensure it continues to be appropriate in light of changing rules. Indeed, U.S. rules require audit committees to review and reassess their charters annually and to have the full board approve any revisions.

As part of their periodic charter review, many committees ask company counsel to check that the charter complies with relevant laws and regulations. They also have management, internal audit, and the external auditors review it to ensure it properly captures their respective interactions with the committee.

Since charters are publicly available, audit committees can easily learn how peer companies capture certain responsibilities and how committee practices are developing in their particular industry.

2 | *Committee evaluations*

The audit committee should periodically evaluate its effectiveness. For many public companies — including those listed on the New York and London stock exchanges — annual assessments of audit committee performance are required.

An audit committee could choose to evaluate its performance by:

- *Comparing its activities against its charter.* This helps the committee confirm it has completed its responsibilities during the year. Timely evaluations allow the committee to take remedial steps in the event an item was missed.

- *Comparing its activities against leading practices.* This helps the committee understand alternative approaches to discharge its responsibilities — ways that might work better. Committee members can learn about leading practices through publications such as this one, surveys and studies, seminars and conferences, and discussions with audit committee members from other companies and external auditors. The key is to adapt any practices you feel would be of benefit for your particular circumstances.

- *Discussing performance among committee members, as well as with management and others.* Committee members have their own views on what works well in the committee and what could improve. Plus, those who interact with the committee — the CEO, the CFO, internal and external auditors, and others — have perspectives on the committee's performance and insights into the issues or areas where the committee should focus more attention. (In some countries, external auditors have to evaluate the audit committee's performance as part of their evaluation of the company's internal control over financial reporting. It's particularly important for the committee to understand if the auditors have any concerns that could affect the auditors' report.)

Many guides are available to assist audit committees in assessing their performance. Appendices A and B include a full assessment guide (which summarizes the practices outlined in this book) and a discussion guide. The American Institute of Certified Public Accountants has an Audit Committee Toolkit that contains a guide. The National Association of Corporate Directors includes an audit committee evaluation tool in *Board Evaluation: Improving Director Effectiveness*.

Many committees have counsel or internal audit coordinate and compile any written surveys completed by the audit committee members. And astute committees work with counsel to ensure the information that is captured and retained is appropriate. Given concerns that assessment results may be "discoverable" in future legal actions, many committees prefer to discuss their performance evaluations instead of completing questionnaires. And many do so in private session.

Informal, ongoing committee evaluation is also important. One committee member noted that at the end of each meeting, the committee briefly discusses what practices worked well during the meeting and what practices could be improved.

Whatever assessment method is used, the objective is to improve the committee's effectiveness. Accordingly, evaluations should focus not only on what the committee does, but also on how effectively it conducts its activities. Committees should engage in thoughtful dialogue rather than viewing their assessment simply as a compliance exercise. Ideally, this dialogue will lead to ideas on how the committee could improve its performance.

The committee should review its assessment results and action plans with the nominating/governance committee or the full board and discuss any additional actions. For example, results could indicate the need for additional training or the need for an additional skill set on the committee, which would necessitate board action.

i. Individual member assessment

Some committees also assess the performance of individual members. Such assessments look at members' objectivity and independence, insight, judgment, communication skills, understanding of the company's business, understanding of the committee's responsibilities, willingness to devote the time necessary to prepare for and participate in the committee's deliberations, and meeting attendance.

Performing individual assessments allows the committee to identify ways in which members could contribute more and what information or assistance they need to do so. One approach is to have each member complete a self-assessment, then discuss results with the committee chair. While some committees have each member assess the other members, that approach is not ideal in such a small group. Indeed, peer evaluations are rarely done even for the entire board.

Whatever approach is selected, the chair should ensure confidentiality of responses and discuss with general counsel what documentation will be created and retained. Perhaps because of the sensitivity of individual member evaluations, it appears few audit committees conduct them.

ii. Frequency of assessment

How often should committees assess their performance? Although many chairs support (and NYSE rules call for) annual evaluations, a wide range of variation exists in practice. For example, some committees evaluate their activities against the charter annually but benchmark against leading practices — at times seeking the perspectives of an outside consultant — every three or four years.

3 | Resources

Audit committees need proper support. On an ongoing basis, they need administrative assistance from the company to schedule meetings, assist with developing agendas, compile and distribute advance materials before meetings, draft minutes, and coordinate responses to the committee's questions. Generally, the committee looks to the corporate secretary, finance department, internal audit director, or a combination to provide this assistance.

Audit committees also may periodically need to engage additional resources in special situations, and it is important they have the authority to do so. The Sarbanes-Oxley Act gives U.S. public companies' audit committees explicit authority to hire independent counsel or other advisors, with the company required to provide appropriate funding for such advisors. Similarly, Canadian Securities Administrators rules give audit committees the authority to engage legal counsel and other advisors as they determine necessary to carry out their duties.

The Society of Corporate Secretaries & Governance Professionals' *Current Board Practices, Sixth Study* found 85% of companies' board committees do not need board approval to engage advisors and to conduct investigations.

Audit committees should specify in the charter their authority to engage external advisors.

4 | *Training and education*

Interview insights

I support the orientation of any new audit committee members, helping them understand the governance processes, key risks, etc.

– IA Director

Audit committee members need appropriate orientation and ongoing training if they are to excel in their oversight role. Education is critical to enable audit committee members not only to understand their responsibilities thoroughly, but also to develop and maintain necessary technical knowledge to discharge them effectively. This means keeping the committee current on regulatory standards and developments, business activities and changes, and other relevant information.

i. New member orientation

New members joining the committee have a special challenge. They need to understand the committee's roles and responsibilities and to become conversant quickly on the financial reports, as well as on the major underlying processes and related risks. If a new committee member doesn't have a financial background, he or she also may benefit from attending accounting or finance programs targeted for directors.

A new audit committee member who also is new to the board needs to understand the company's business and industry plus key business risks, and so should participate in a broader orientation program. The Society of Corporate Secretaries & Governance Professionals' *Current Board Practices, Sixth Study* indicates that while 60% of companies have a formal orientation program for new directors, only 22% have a separate orientation for new audit committee members.

Orientation programs should be conducted timely and cover the topics sufficiently. Exhibit 9.2 provides topics that an orientation program might cover.

Exhibit 9.2	Potential topics for orientation programs

Financial reporting and control reporting

Standard financial reports: Information that flows through to financial reports, what key line items represent, and how to read reports and recognize issues

Critical accounting policies: What they are, why they were selected, the level of estimation involved in their determination, and their impact on financial reports

Areas involving a high degree of judgment: Which areas require the use of estimates and how they can impact reported results

Internal control over financial reporting: The control environment, security and integrity of information systems, how management addresses key risks (including fraud risk), how management monitors control effectiveness, public reports on internal control, and status of control deficiencies

Earnings trends: Financial position and prospects of the company, as well as analysts' expectations and the achievability of forecasts

Financing and liquidity: The company's debt and financing structure, availability of capital, and timing of near-term refinancing

Other responsibilities

Statutory and regulatory requirements: Nature of such requirements; background of current issues, including restrictions placed on the company and on the audit committee

Compliance: Elements of the compliance program and the committee's oversight role

Whistleblower program: Procedures for handling complaints about accounting, internal control, or auditing matters; reporting to the committee; and whistleblower history/experience

Code of conduct: Provisions; how it is communicated and enforced

Legal issues: Legal matters that could have financial reporting implications

Audit committee processes

The committee's charter: Outline of key responsibilities and authority

Meeting schedule and agendas: Meeting frequency, length, and typical topics

Support and resources: Who supports the committee

Committee assessment: Self-assessment and charter review processes

Chair: Role, special activities, and reporting to full committee and to board

Key relationships

Management: Identity of key finance and business unit management, backgrounds, and experience

Internal audit: Responsibilities, capabilities, reporting relationship with the committee, nature of audit plans, and reports

External auditors: Relationship with the committee, audit scope, and reports

Others: Identity and credentials of other key personnel reporting periodically to the committee (e.g., chief compliance officer, chief risk officer, ethics officer, legal counsel)

Orientation programs can be open to all members — indeed, some veteran committee members may find participating in such sessions with newer members helpful.

ii. Ongoing development

An ongoing training program allows members to stay current with significant changes in the company, such as acquisitions or expansion into new lines of business. As well as understanding the impact of changes within the company, committees need to understand the impact of governance, accounting, and regulatory developments. Exhibit 9.3 shows some of the more important ongoing training and education needs.

Exhibit 9.3	Information that helps audit committee members stay current

- Regular updates on accounting and reporting developments. To be most relevant, these briefings should be limited to matters most likely to impact the company. For example, how will impending changes in standards affect the company, and how does management plan to deal with them, including their impact on internal control?

- Periodic briefings by the company's business units on operational as well as financial performance. This information helps committee members understand and assess business units' financial results. Such briefings are particularly relevant when a company has acquired or expanded into new businesses or shifted its strategic focus. Many committees find it useful to hold these discussions at operating locations.

- Briefings on key support departments or cross-business-unit issues. These are useful when significant changes are under way. Subjects could include new information systems implementation or the company's risk management program. It is important that presenters tailor these briefings to the needs of committee members.

- Targeted sessions on special risk areas. Audit committees can benefit from briefings on complex and company- or industry-specific areas such as off balance sheet structures and hedging programs. For example, audit committees of financial institutions will find information useful on technical areas such as loan loss reserves, foreign currency trading, and financial derivatives.

- Sessions on changing corporate governance standards, particularly as they relate to the audit committee itself. Committees need to understand proposed rules so they can proactively consider actions needed and timing.

Committees can meet their training and development objectives a number of ways:

- *Customized in-house sessions.* Whether developed by management or external parties, these can be particularly effective if tailored to the issues the committee and company face. Such sessions also allow members to discuss specific concerns, including ones that may be highly confidential. The sessions can be open to other directors who are interested. Anecdotal evidence suggests many directors are taking audit committees up on offers to attend these sessions — recognizing the need to know more about financial reporting.

- *Director conferences.* These programs feature leading authorities and seasoned directors who provide insights on current issues and share their practical experience. Participants get the opportunity to understand what their fellow directors are thinking and how other boards are addressing specific issues — making the programs a great setting for sharing leading practice ideas.

- *External auditors' programs.* Many external audit firms have special programs for audit committee members, as well as providing courses on accounting and financial reporting. These provide an opportunity to learn from subject matter experts and to interact with fellow audit committee members.

Many audit committee members find it valuable to attend meetings of other board committees and to interact with other directors and management to gain insight into other aspects of the company's operations.

Ongoing development and education sessions may occur as part of regular committee meetings, which could expand the meeting duration. Some committees schedule separate training sessions to allow for adequate time and focus on these educational topics. The approach a committee selects depends on the number of participants (audit committee versus other directors also attending) and logistical issues in assembling the committee for a separate session.

Some audit committees set goals each year for continuing education — both in-house and external sessions. And they ask committee members who attend outside programs to share their key takeaways with the committee upon their return.

Some committees take an integrated approach to understanding issues in the company. *For example, for each major area or function in the company:*

- The business unit manager discusses what is going on in the business

- A manager from the finance department describes how the business is accounted for, financial reporting risks, and how the operation's results translate into numbers in the financial reports

- Internal audit discusses its plans to conduct an audit of the area, as well as key findings from prior audits

- The external auditors explain how they view the risks to the financial statements for the business and describe their audit scope

This integrated approach to ongoing education not only informs the audit committee, but also allows members to ask questions and get to the bottom of issues with all relevant parties in the room.

Each committee needs to decide for itself how best to stay current, given the dynamic environment in which companies operate. Defining and agreeing upon a plan for ongoing training will help a committee to best position itself to address the changes.

Appendix A
Audit Committee Self-assessment Guide

The following guide summarizes leading audit committee practices discussed in this report. You may use it to help assess your audit committee's performance and identify changes to consider in your processes. Audit committees may also find it beneficial to obtain feedback from management, the internal audit director, general counsel, and the external auditors on committee performance.

Characteristics of Effective Audit Committees	Comments and Follow-up Actions (including any personal plans)
Financial Reporting and Disclosures **Your committee:** Adequately understands the company's **business** and the **industry** in which it operates	
Is satisfied the company adequately **addresses** the **risk** that the financial statements may be **materially misstated**, intentionally or unintentionally	
Understands how management and the external auditors **evaluate materiality**, both **quantitatively** and **qualitatively**, for financial reporting purposes	
Assesses **reasonableness** and **appropriateness** of **critical accounting policies** the company follows, discussing with management and external auditors	
Reviews the **reasons** for and **implications** of **changes** in **accounting principles** made at **management's discretion**, understanding stakeholders' potential reaction before approving	
Scrutinizes areas involving **management estimates** that have a material impact on the financial statements and understands the reasonableness of the **underlying assumptions** and whether the amount recorded is closer to the **conservative or aggressive** end of the spectrum	

Characteristics of Effective Audit Committees	Comments and Follow-up Actions (including any personal plans)
Discusses with management *substantive reasons* for *significant changes* in the financial statements — between reporting periods and from budget — ensuring *explanations* are *consistent* with *understanding* of the company's *performance*	
Reviews with management transactions that are *unusual, complex*, or have increased volume near period ends and their *accounting treatment*, evaluating *appropriateness* and *consistency* with members' *knowledge* of the company	
Understands management's process to identify any significant *related party transactions* that occur during a reporting period and is satisfied with the related disclosures	
Reads *annual financial statements*, assessing their *completeness and consistency* with operational and other information known to members and discussing also with management and the external auditors	
Reviews *interim financial statements* and related disclosures, understanding consistency with annual reporting, *before filing* with regulators	
Understands and is comfortable with *press releases* and other *financial information* (e.g., earnings guidance, forward-looking information, information for rating agencies) routinely *disclosed* by the company, including separate reporting of *special items* or *non-GAAP* disclosures	
Reads, before publication, *narrative reporting* and related information, ensuring *consistency* with *financial statements, completeness*, and appropriate *transparency* for issues such as *liquidity and financing needs*	

Characteristics of Effective Audit Committees	Comments and Follow-up Actions (including any personal plans)
Discusses **audit results** with **external auditors**, considering management's handling of corrected or **uncorrected misstatements**	
Meets periodically with **counsel** to discuss **litigation, claims, contingencies,** or other **significant issues** and their **impact** on the financial statements	
Understands how management captures **all relevant information** in the financial statements, including how the **management disclosure committee** functions	
Reviews any correspondence between the company and **regulators** regarding financial statement filings and disclosures	
Considers the impact of any identified **subsequent events** on financial disclosures	
Risk Management and the System of Internal Control **Your committee:** Is comfortable with the **effectiveness** of the company's **risk management** process	
Clearly **understands** and agrees with the board on **which** of the **key risks** — likely those covering financial reporting and compliance with laws and regulations — **it oversees** on behalf of the board. Agrees with the board on the **specific scope** of the committee's oversight responsibilities for **monitoring risks.**	

Characteristics of Effective Audit Committees	Comments and Follow-up Actions (including any personal plans)
Reviews the *approach* to and *extent* of *internal control testing by management, internal audit*, and *external auditors* and how the testing supports any related *reporting* the company does	
Discusses with management, internal audit, and external auditors their *observations, issues*, and *findings* on *internal control effectiveness*. Understands any *significant* or *material control weaknesses* as well as management's plans to *remediate* any *control deficiencies*.	
Reads management's *external reports* on the *effectiveness* of internal control and/or risk management and any related reports from external auditors	
Understands whether *compensation incentives* could create *risk* for financial reporting	
Understands any factors that *increase financial reporting fraud* risk and how management addresses the risk	
Understands the risks of *bribery* and *corruption* and how management is minimizing those risks	
Culture and Compliance *Your committee:* Evaluates the *"tone at the top"* and the *company's culture*, understanding their relevance to financial reporting and compliance	

Characteristics of Effective Audit Committees	Comments and Follow-up Actions (including any personal plans)
Understands the effectiveness of the company's *programs* for ensuring *compliance with laws and regulations*, considers any *significant compliance issues* identified, and is satisfied with management's *actions*	
Ensures management has an *appropriate code of conduct*. Makes sure that management provides the code, along with *related training*, to employees and periodically requires employees to *certify* their *compliance*.	
Is satisfied that the company's *ethics* and *conduct policies* properly address *culturally* or *regionally sensitive* issues	
Sees that appropriate *support channels* are *available* to help employees address *compliance* and *ethics issues*	
Meets periodically with internal audit, general counsel, the *compliance officer*, and management, among others, to discuss sensitive issues	
Ensures procedures are in place to *receive, retain*, and *address complaints* regarding accounting, internal controls, or auditing matters. Considers the potential impact and resolution of any significant issues raised through the *whistleblower* program.	
Oversight of Management and Internal Audit *Your committee:* Maintains a *productive relationship* with management through open lines of communication and *candid, continual dialogue*, including between committee meetings	

Characteristics of Effective Audit Committees	Comments and Follow-up Actions (including any personal plans)
Strikes the *right balance* between *advising* management and *monitoring* management and is ready to *increase* its *engagement* if changes in circumstances warrant	
Ensures management obtains the *audit committee's input* before making *key decisions*	
Assesses senior finance management's *performance* and *competence*, obtaining feedback from internal audit and external auditors	
Monitors *succession plans* for the *CFO* and senior finance team members	
Involves management appropriately in *meetings* and ensures *emphasis* on *discussion*, not presentation	
Meets privately with management on a *regular* basis	
Builds a *trusting relationship* with *internal audit* that includes *candid* and *continual communication* between meetings, facilitating ability to raise sensitive issues	
Ensures the role internal audit plays *meets* the *committee's needs* for assurance and provides *value* to *management*	

Characteristics of Effective Audit Committees	Comments and Follow-up Actions (including any personal plans)
Approves internal audit's *charter* and reviews *annual plans* and any *significant changes* — ensuring appropriate coverage of risks and coordination of work with external auditors	
Ensures internal audit has *adequate resources* and *budget*, including quality and continuity of *staff*, with ability to supplement skills as needed	
Discusses *significant* internal audit *findings*, reported to the committee at an appropriately *summarized* level, as well as the *status* of management's remediation actions	
Ensures internal audit *reports directly* to the *committee*, as well as to an appropriately *senior position* within the company, promoting internal audit's stature and *objectivity*	
Plays a *central role* in *appointing* or replacing the *internal audit director, evaluating* his or her *performance* and *determining compensation*	
Evaluates internal audit's *performance* and operational *independence* by weighing results of any quality control reviews as well as feedback from management and external auditors	
Meets privately with the internal audit director on a *regular* basis	
Relationship with External Auditors *Your committee:* Builds a *trusting* and *professional relationship* with external auditors, ensuring *open* lines of *communication*	

Characteristics of Effective Audit Committees	Comments and Follow-up Actions (including any personal plans)
Drives the *selection, oversight*, and *evaluation* of external auditors, obtaining management's and internal audit's input and considering replacement when appropriate	
Ensures external auditors' *independence* by *preapproving* audit and nonaudit *services*, understanding impact of fees, and evaluating type of *nonaudit services*	
Reviews the *external audit scope*, understanding *risk coverage* and significant plan changes	
Receives *information required* to be *communicated* under *auditing* and *regulatory standards* and seeks insight on how the company's practices compare to those of peers	
Reviews *management's representation letters* to the auditors and inquires about any nonstandard representations	
Understands any *disagreements* between the auditors and management and determines whether *outside advice* is needed for *resolution*	
Understands management's rationale for *using other audit firms* for audit work or other services	
Meets privately with external auditors on a *regular* basis	

Characteristics of Effective Audit Committees	Comments and Follow-up Actions (including any personal plans)
What to Do When Things Go Wrong *Your committee:* Understands any significant *identified errors* in previously issued financial statements and agrees with management conclusions regarding the need for *restatement*	
Ensures management conducts a *thorough investigation* to identify and resolve all errors	
Understands its *role* and key considerations in overseeing *investigations* (for possible fraud or illegal acts) and is prepared to *take charge* when needed	
Has *authority* and makes the appropriate decision on whether to engage *outside advisors*	
Actively *monitors* investigation progress and ensures management captures *lessons learned* and applies them in future investigations	
Is satisfied a *crisis management plan* exists and enables the company to *respond quickly* and appropriately to an emerging crisis	
Committee Composition *Your committee:* Has its *new members* selected by the *nominating committee* based on *skills* and *attributes* the committee needs	
Considers, with the nominating committee, a need for *balancing continuity* with *fresh perspective* when addressing member turnover	

Characteristics of Effective Audit Committees	Comments and Follow-up Actions (including any personal plans)
Has a *succession plan* for its members and chair	
Has a *chair* who possesses *strong leadership* qualities, ability to promote effective discussion and working relationships, and *time* and *financial expertise* to direct the committee appropriately	
Has *members* who *possess* critical *characteristics* such as integrity, courage, skepticism, independent judgment, and industry knowledge and have the available *time*	
Has members who are *independent* and possess requisite levels of *financial literacy* and financial *expertise*	
Is the *right size*, bringing requisite knowledge, abilities, and skills to the table, yet *small enough* to *act cohesively*	
Meetings *Your committee:* Uses a *scheduling calendar* to ensure it *addresses all* its *responsibilities* over the course of a year, while balancing its workload	
Holds a *sufficient number* of meetings, *scheduled at appropriate points*, to address its responsibilities on a timely basis	
Ensures meetings are of *adequate length* to allow the committee to accomplish its agenda, with *time* to *fully discuss* issues	

Characteristics of Effective Audit Committees	Comments and Follow-up Actions (including any personal plans)
Plans meetings properly — with the *chair driving* the *agenda* and members providing input	
Is satisfied it receives appropriate *advance material* for agenda topics, providing the *right* information and *insight*, and that material is received in a *timely* manner and *reviewed* by *members* before meetings	
Requires meeting attendance by the *right individuals*, those with *meaningful input* on agenda items, and *limits* the number of *observers* whose presence may hinder discussion	
Meets in separate *private sessions regularly* with the *CFO, internal audit director*, and *external auditors* and periodically with *general counsel*, *compliance officer, chief risk officer*, and other management — allowing *full* and *frank discussion* of potentially sensitive matters	
Has members meet *regularly* in *private session*, allowing *confidential discussion* of management's and auditors' performance and reflection on other issues	
Communicates effectively with management about issues that arise between meetings, thereby avoiding surprises	
Allows time at meetings for dialogue, with the discussion focusing on relevant topics	
Ensures *minutes* provide *accurate descriptions* of meetings, at the *right level* of *detail*, and reviews and approves them in a timely manner	

Characteristics of Effective Audit Committees	Comments and Follow-up Actions (including any personal plans)
Reports regularly to the *board* to discuss *activities,* key *issues, major recommendations*, and action plans	
Supporting Committee Effectiveness *Your committee:* Has a *written charter*, which has been *approved* by the *board* of directors, that it *assesses* annually for any *updates*	
Ensures annually that it has *carried out all* the *responsibilities* outlined in its charter	
Assesses *performance* of the *committee* as a *whole* annually, taking decisive corrective action and considering improvements	
Evaluates individual members' performance regularly, considering training and other needed support	
Has proper *administrative support* on an ongoing basis and the *authority* to engage *additional resources* when needed	
Ensures *new members* receive *robust orientation* to enable them to understand their role and get up to speed quickly	
Ensures that *all members* have access to *continuing education* on business and accounting developments and other matters relevant to new responsibilities or changes in the business	

Appendix B
Discussion Guide for Assessing Performance

An audit committee can use this guide to facilitate dialogue about possible ways to improve its performance. While Appendix A links to the many leading practices covered in the book, some committees prefer to assess their performance using discussion among members. The committee also should consider obtaining feedback from management, the internal audit director, general counsel, and external auditors.

1. How are we making sure we appropriately focus our review of financial reporting on the higher-risk areas — that either require significant management judgment or are more susceptible to error or fraud?

2. What higher-risk areas should we devote more attention to? What lower-risk topics are we spending disproportionate time on, and so should consider handling differently?

3. Do the briefing materials allow us to easily understand the issues and the context for the topics being covered in the meetings, or does the volume of material detract from the core messages? What additional or different information should we get?

4. What could we do differently in meetings to improve the substance of the discussion? Do we need longer or additional meetings?

5. How do we ensure we have the right level of engagement with management to allow us to understand management's competence and ethical standards? Would the CFO be able to stand up to pressure from other executives if they inappropriately push for certain results?

6. What actions can we take to improve our relationships with internal audit and the external auditors?

7. What are some ways we could improve the private sessions to encourage a more open and robust dialogue?

8. Are we getting the needed support from internal and external resources?

9. What additional skills or experience would be useful to have on our committee? Can these be developed through training, or should we add a new member?

10. Which other board committees (e.g., compensation committee) have responsibilities that intersect with our scope? How are we coordinating with them to address issues of mutual interest?

Appendix C
Required Communications from the External Auditors

The audit committee needs to understand a number of factors about the external auditors, the audit, the results of audit work, and the financial reporting process to have assurance in the financial statements it oversees. And it needs that information on a sufficiently timely basis to enable it to take appropriate action, if needed. Accordingly, the external auditors should inform the audit committee about these items before issuing their audit report. In recognizing how important this information is, auditing standard setters have mandated a number of communications. This appendix summarizes the International Standards on Auditing communication requirements, then the additional requirements in the United States, and the proposed (at the time of this publication) requirements by the Public Company Accounting Oversight Board (PCAOB).

1 | International Standards on Auditing requirements

Auditors should communicate with the audit committee on a timely basis. The appropriate timing of the communications will vary with each audit engagement. For example, communications regarding planning may be made early in the audit engagement, and it may be appropriate to communicate a significant difficulty encountered during the audit as soon as practicable if it is likely to lead to a modified audit opinion. Additionally, the auditors should provide significant findings from their audit in writing if — in their professional judgment — oral communication would not be adequate. This may be the case if there are significant disagreements with management relating to the application of accounting principles, the basis for management's judgment concerning accounting estimates, the severity of a control deficiency, or the wording of the auditors' report. For such disagreements, the auditors' communication should include the nature of the disagreement; its accounting, auditing, or reporting significance; the persons involved; and how the matter was resolved.

International standards require auditors to communicate a number of specific items, as follows.

Auditor independence:
- A statement that the engagement team and others in the firm, as appropriate, have complied with relevant ethical requirements regarding independence.

- A list of all relationships and other matters between the auditors and the company that in the auditors' professional judgment may reasonably be thought to bear on independence, including total fees charged during the period covered by the financial statements for audit and non-audit services allocated to appropriate categories.

- If threats to the auditors' independence have been identified, the related safeguards the auditors have applied to eliminate or reduce the threats to an acceptable level.

Responsibilities:
- The auditors' responsibilities in relation to the financial statement audit, including the responsibility for forming and expressing an opinion on the financial statements prepared by management with the oversight of the audit committee.
- The fact that the financial statement audit does not relieve management or the audit committee of their respective responsibilities.
- The auditors should evaluate whether the two-way communications with the audit committee have been adequate to support the audit objectives.

Additional suggested communications or commentary

Communicating the auditors' responsibilities helps establish effective two-way communication. When the auditors' purpose is clear, the auditors and the audit committee have a better mutual understanding of relevant issues and the expected actions arising from the communication process. The expectation is that communication will be two-way and the audit committee members will communicate with the auditors matters they consider relevant to the audit — for example, any suspicion or detection of fraud and concerns about the integrity or competence of senior management.

The auditors' and management's responsibilities are often documented in an engagement letter. The audit committee may find it useful to receive a copy of this letter.

Audit strategy and timing:
- An overview of the planned scope and timing of the audit.

Additional suggested communications or commentary

This may include how the auditors propose to address the significant risks of material misstatement, whether due to fraud or error, and planned use of the company's internal audit function or other parties.

Difficulties encountered in performing the audit:
- Any significant difficulties encountered during the audit. Significant difficulties encountered during the audit may include such matters as significant delays in management providing required information.

Significant matters discussed with management and written representation:
- Significant matters arising from the audit that were discussed with management.
- Written representations the auditors are requesting.

Additional suggested communications or commentary

Concerns about management's consultations with other accountants on accounting or auditing matters.

Discussions or correspondence in connection with the initial or recurring appointment of the auditor regarding accounting practices, the application of auditing standards, or fees for audit or other services.

Accounting policies, practices, and estimates:

* Views about significant qualitative aspects of the company's accounting practices, including accounting policies, accounting estimates, and financial statement disclosures. When applicable, explain why the auditors consider a significant accounting practice that is acceptable under the applicable financial reporting framework not to be most appropriate to the particular circumstances of the company.

Additional suggested communications or commentary

These communications may include such matters as the appropriateness of the accounting policies for the company's particular circumstances, considering the need to balance the cost of providing information with the likely benefit to the users of the company's financial statements. Where acceptable alternative accounting policies exist, identify the financial statement items that are affected by the choice of significant accounting policies as well as information on accounting policies used by similar companies.

The initial selection of and changes in significant accounting policies, including the application of new accounting standards.

The effect of significant accounting policies in controversial or emerging areas for which there is a lack of authoritative guidance.

The effect of the timing of transactions in relation to the period in which they are recorded.

For significant estimates, describe the process used by management, the risks of material misstatement, indicators of possible management bias, and how the estimation uncertainty is disclosed in the financial statements.

The issues involved, and related judgments made, in formulating particularly sensitive financial statement disclosures.

The potential effect on the financial statements of significant risks, exposures, and uncertainties, such as pending litigation, that are disclosed in the financial statements.

The extent to which the financial statements are affected by unusual transactions, including nonrecurring amounts recognized during the period, and the extent to which such transactions are separately disclosed in the financial statements.

Other matters:

* Other matters arising from the audit that, in the auditors' professional judgment, are significant to the oversight of the financial reporting process.

Additional suggested communications or commentary

Other significant matters may include such matters as material misstatements of fact or material inconsistencies in information accompanying the audited financial statements that have been corrected.

Corrected and uncorrected misstatements:

* Uncorrected misstatements and the effect that they, individually or in aggregate, may have on the opinion in the auditors' report, identifying any material uncorrected misstatements individually.

* The effect of uncorrected misstatements related to prior periods on the relevant classes of transactions, account balances or disclosures, and the financial statements as a whole.

* Any request that uncorrected misstatements be corrected.

Going concern:

- Events or conditions identified that may cast significant doubt on the company's ability to continue as a going concern. Also whether the events or conditions constitute a material uncertainty, whether the use of the going concern assumption is appropriate in the preparation and presentation of the financial statements, and the adequacy of related disclosures.

Fraud and illegal acts:

- Fraud involving company management, business unit management, employees who have significant roles in companywide controls, or others where the fraud resulted in a material misstatement of the company's financial statements.

Other information in documents containing audited financial information:

- The auditors need to notify the audit committee if there is a material misstatement of fact in such other information that management refuses to correct.

Related parties

- Significant matters arising during the audit in connection with the company's related parties.

2 | Additional communications required in the United States

U.S. auditing standards require auditors to make certain communications in addition to those required by the International Standards on Auditing.

Auditor independence:

- All relationships between the auditors and the company or persons in financial reporting oversight roles at the company. Any additional independence matters that have occurred or have been identified subsequent to the communication about independence provided during the audit planning phase. The auditors' independence obligation encompasses not only an obligation to satisfy the independence criteria set out in the rules and standards, but also an obligation to satisfy all other independence criteria applicable to the engagement, including the independence criteria set out in the rules and regulations of the U.S. Securities and Exchange Commission (SEC) under the federal securities laws.

Audit strategy:

- The terms of the engagement and significant changes and limitations to the planned strategy.

Auditor appointment:

- Any significant issues that were discussed with management in connection with the appointment or retention of the auditors, including any discussions regarding the application of accounting principles and auditing standards. (For example, a difference between the viewpoints of the new auditors and the predecessor auditors.)

Accounting policies:

- The initial selection of and changes in significant accounting policies, including the application of new accounting standards and the effect of significant accounting policies in controversial or emerging areas for which there is a lack of authoritative guidance.

- Alternative treatments for accounting policies and practices related to material items, including recognition, measurement, presentation, and disclosure alternatives that have been discussed with management during the current audit period; the ramifications of the use of such alternative disclosures and treatments; and the treatment preferred by the auditors. If auditor requested changes to significant accounting practices are not made, the impact on the financial statements of the current and future years, including the audit report.

Accounting estimates:

- The basis for the auditors' conclusion regarding the reasonableness of the accounting estimate.

Uncorrected misstatements:

- Uncorrected misstatements aggregated by the auditors and determined by management to be immaterial.

Going concern:

- If the auditors extended their procedures as part of the audit, including results and conclusions.

Weaknesses in internal control:

- Any significant deficiencies or material weaknesses in the design or operation of internal control over financial reporting that came to the auditors' attention.

Disagreements with management:

- Any disagreements with management, whether or not satisfactorily resolved, about matters that individually or in the aggregate could be significant to the financial statements, management's assessment of internal control over financial reporting, the effectiveness of internal control, or the auditors' report.

Other information in documents containing audited financial information:

- The external auditors' responsibility for other information in documents containing audited financial statements, such as management's discussion and analysis.

Outside communication:

- Significant accounting matters for which the auditors have consulted outside the engagement team.

Fees (SEC-registered companies only):

- The total fees the auditors charged during the period covered by the financial statements for audit and non-audit services during the current and prior years, including a description of the types of services rendered, by category.

Quality control procedures (New York Stock Exchange companies only):

- The report on the audit firm's quality control.

3 | *Additional guidance under the PCAOB's proposed rule: Audit Committee Communications*

At the time of this publication, the PCAOB has issued a proposed standard, *Communications with Audit Committees*, with the objective of enhancing communications between auditors and audit committees. The list below describes certain additional items the PCAOB proposes to require.

Auditors' appointment or retention:
- The auditor should discuss with the audit committee any significant issues discussed with management in connection with the appointment or retention of the auditor, including any discussions regarding the application of accounting principles and auditing standards.

Mutual understanding:
- The objective of the audit, the responsibilities of the auditors, and the responsibilities of management, which are to be recorded in an engagement letter that is provided to the audit committee annually. The roles, responsibilities, and location of firms participating in the audit and whether persons with specialized skills are needed to perform the audit. The auditors need to evaluate whether the two-way communications with the audit committee have been adequate to support the audit objectives.

- The basis for the auditor's determination that he or she can serve as principal auditor.

Accounting policies:
- If information is not adequately described by management, the auditors should communicate any omitted or inadequately described matters.

Accounting estimates:
- The process used by management in forming particularly sensitive accounting estimates and how much estimates are subsequently monitored by management. Management's significant assumptions used in significant accounting estimates that have a high degree of subjectivity. Any significant changes to assumptions or processes made by management to the significant accounting estimates in the year under audit, a description of the reasons for the changes, the effects on the financial statements, and the information that supports or challenges such changes. When an estimate involves a range of possible outcomes, communicate what the impact of changes within the range would be to the estimate and whether there is a risk of material misstatement.

Corrected misstatements:
- Corrected misstatements that might not have been detected except through the auditing procedures performed, including the implications such corrected misstatements might have on the financial reporting process.

Other matters:
- Whether the auditors are aware of other matters that may relate to the audit, including complaints or concerns raised regarding accounting or auditing matters.

Appendix D
Project Method

This report is based on interviews, a review of literature and relevant surveys, and the knowledge and experience of PwC professionals.

Literature search

The project team reviewed literature and surveys on audit committee-related topics, focusing on information published since 2005. The team also reviewed information available on websites that focus on corporate governance. Some of the key sources we drew on for this report are listed in Appendix E.

Interview activities

We conducted interviews with 36 audit committee chairs and corporate governance thought leaders from Australia, Canada, China/Hong Kong, Germany, India, the Middle East, the Netherlands, Russia, Singapore, South Africa, and the United States. Additionally, we conducted interviews with 44 internal audit directors from Australia, Brazil, China/Hong Kong, France, Germany, India, the Middle East, the Netherlands, Russia, Singapore, South Africa, and the United States.

We acknowledge and greatly appreciate all of these individuals who gave their time and shared their experiences, expertise, and perspectives. The views expressed in this report are those of PwC, unless otherwise indicated.

Among the audit committee chairs and thought leaders interviewed are:

Name	Affiliations
Mahmood Al-Kooheji	Apicorp
Jamie Allen	Founding Secretary General of the Asian Corporate Governance Association
Subodh Bhargava	Tata Steel Limited, Glaxosmithkline Consumer Healthcare Limited, Samtel Color Limited, Carborundum Universal Limited
Iain Bruce	Noble Group Limited
Leslie A. Brun	Merck & Co., Inc., Broadridge Financial Solutions Inc., Automatic Data Processing, Inc. (ADP)
His Excellency Hamad Buamim	Dubai World, Emirates NBD Bank PJSC, Union Properties PJSC
John Buchanan	Business Connexion Group Limited, Aspen Pharmacare

Name	Affiliations
Naresh Chandra	The Naresh Chandra Committee on Corporate Governance, Balrampur Chini Mills Limited, Ambuja Cements Limited, Bajaj Holdings & Investment Limited, Bajaj Finserv Limited, Bajaj Auto Limited, Eros International PLC, Cairn India Limited, Vedanta Resources PLC, Electrosteel Castings Limited, ACC Limited, Hindustan Motors Limited, Gammon Infrastructure Projects Limited, AVTEC Limited, Vis Legis Consult Private Limited
John Clappison	Cameco Corp., Canadian REIT, Inmet Mining Corporation, Rogers Communications Inc., Sun Life Financial Inc.
Jennifer Clark	Defence Materiel Organisation, National ICT Australia
Rick Cottrell	Glenrand MIB Limited
Clayton C. Daley Jr.	Foster Wheeler AG, Starwood Hotel & Resorts Worldwide, Nucor Corporation
Peter Day	SAI Global Limited
Amal Ganguli	Maruti Suzuki India Limited, New Delhi Television Limited, Tata Communications Limited
Jane Harvey	IOOF Holdings Limited, Medibank Private, State Government of Victoria - Department of Treasury and Finance
Hester Hickey	Metorex Limited, Omnia Holdings Limited
Eric Hooper	Synergy
Professor Mervyn King	Chairman of the King Committee on Corporate Governance in South Africa, First Vice President of the Institute of Directors Southern Africa, Chairman of the Global Reporting Initiative in Amsterdam, Member of the Private Sector Advisory Group to the World Bank on Corporate Governance, Deputy Chairman of the International Integrated Reporting Committee in London, Chairman of the Integrated Reporting Committee in South Africa, Expert Adviser to the Finance and Audit Committee on the work of the Office of the Inspector General in Geneva, Chaired the United Nations Committee on Governance and Oversight, Honorary Fellow of the Institute of Internal Auditors United Kingdom and Ireland and of CPA Australia (Certified Practising Accountants)
Mary Mogford	Potash Corporation of Saskatchewan Inc., Nordion Inc.
Ton Nelissen	APG Groep, Kamer van Koophandel Nederland
Thomas O'Neill	Bell Canada Enterprises and Bell Canada, Adecco S.A., Loblaw Companies Limited, Nexen Inc., The Bank of Nova Scotia
Nigel Payne	Bidvest Group Limited, Bidvest Bank Limited, BSI Steel Limited, Glenrand MIB Limited, Mr Price Group Limited, Johannesburg Stock Exchange, PPS Insurance, STRATE Limited

Name	Affiliations
Ian Renard	CSL Limited
Deepak M. Satwalekar	Infosys Technologies Limited
Rory Scott	Dimension Data Holdings Limited
Richard Sheath	Eurochem Group
T. Brian Stevenson	MTR Corporation Limited
Klaus Sturany	Bayer AG, Sulzer AG, Hannover Rueckversicherung AG, Heidelberger Druckmaschinen AG, ÖIAG
Lawrence A. Weinbach	Avon Products, Inc., Discover Financial Services, Inc.
Dr. Kelvin Wong, FHKIoD	Chairman of The Hong Kong Institute of Directors

Among the internal audit directors interviewed are:

Name	Company
Crystal Abdoll	PetroSA (Pty) Limited
Fatima Ally	Total SA (Pty) Limited
Douglas J. Anderson	The Dow Chemical Company
Jeff Bodner	Intel Corporation
Darren Box	Centrelink
David Cheung	Ping An Insurance (Group) Co. of China Limited
Gerry Chicoine	AT&T, Inc.
Bertrand Delahaye	SAFRAN
Mohamed Dukandar	Telkom SA Limited
JinXiong Feng	China Eastern Airlines Corporation Limited
Melvin Flowers	Microsoft Corporation
Johan Goosen	Lonmin PLC
Norman Gray	MassMart Holdings Limited
Brent Green	Macquarie Group Limited
Gregory T. Grocholski	The Dow Chemical Company
Alexey Guriev	TNK-BP International Limited

Name	Company
Samuel Hanhua Zhang	China Mobile Communications Corporation
Bryan Harris	Aluminium Bahrain
Nick Hirons	GlaxoSmithKline
Michael Holtmann	E.ON AG
Amanda Hoosen	Hollard Insurance Company Limited
Joe Ioculano	Mubadala Development Company PJSC
Fang Lan	China Eastern Airlines Corporation Limited
Douglas Lui	The Hongkong and Shanghai Hotels, Limited
Kevin McCabe	Wells Fargo & Co.
Luiz Umberto Modenese	Cielo (Visa Group)
Andre Nortier	Sanlam Limited
Nagesh Pinge	Tata Motors Limited
Shamini Ramalingam	Bharti Airtel Limted
Jean-François Sautin	Lafarge Group
Marius Schafer	Business Connexion
N.G. Shankar	Aditya Birla Group
Lucy Sheng	Ehouse
Lee Sullivan	Insurance Australia Group
Rinus van der Struis	Rabobank Group

Appendix E
Selected Bibliography and Sources

The following is a selection of key sources, including reports and surveys from which we drew:

Association of Certified Fraud Examiners, *Report to the Nations on Occupational Fraud and Abuse: 2010 Global Fraud Study*, 2010.

Center for Audit Quality, *Deterring and Detecting Financial Reporting Fraud*, 2010.

Committee of Sponsoring Organizations of the Treadway Commission, *Enterprise Risk Management — Integrated Framework, Executive Summary and Framework*, 2004.

Committee of Sponsoring Organizations of the Treadway Commission, *Internal Control — Integrated Framework*, 1992.

The Conference Board, *Corporate Governance Handbook — Legal Standards and Board Practices,* 3rd ed., 2009.

The Conference Board, in collaboration with the Society of Corporate Secretaries & Governance Professionals, *The 2010 U.S. Directors' Compensation and Board Practices Report*, 2010.

The Institute of Internal Auditors, *2010 Global Audit Information Network* survey, 2010.

National Association of Corporate Directors, *2010 NACD Public Company Governance Survey*, 2010.

PwC, *Confronting corruption, The business case for an effective anti-corruption programme,* 2008.

PwC, *2009 Global Economic Crime Survey*, 2009.

PwC, *2010 Annual Corporate Directors Survey*, 2010.

PwC, *2011 State of the Internal Audit Profession Study*, 2011.

Society of Corporate Secretaries & Governance Professionals, *Current Board Practices, Sixth Study*, 2008.

Spencer Stuart, *Spencer Stuart Board Index 2010*, 2010.

Transparency International, *2008 Bribe Payers Index*, 2008.

Transparency International, *2010 Global Perceptions Index*, 2010.

Weil Gotshal & Manges, LLP, *International Comparison of Selected Corporate Governance Guidelines and Codes of Best Practice*, September 2008.

These websites provide access to useful information:

American Institute of Certified Public Accountants' Audit Committee Effectiveness Center: www.aicpa.org/audcommctr

Committee of Sponsoring Organizations of the Treadway Commission (COSO): www.coso.org

The Conference Board Governance Center: www.conference-board.org/governance

European Corporate Governance Institute: www.ecgi.org

Institute of Corporate Directors: www.icd.ca

Institute of Directors: www.iod.com

The Institute of Internal Auditors: www.theiia.org

National Association of Corporate Directors: www.nacdonline.org

PwC: www.pwc.com/us/centerforboardgovernance

Keyword Index

The IIA Research Foundation
Donor Recognition

The Institute of Internal Auditors Research Foundation would not be able to function without its valuable donors, and thanks the volunteers and contributors who make its successes possible, including the following:

For sponsoring this publication:

PwC
IIA–Chicago Chapter
IIA–Philadelphia Chapter

Research Foundation Donor Recognition

Strategic Principal Partners
ACL Services Ltd.
CCH® TeamMate

Principal Partners
CaseWare IDEA Inc.
Ernst & Young LLP
PwC

Research Sponsors
IIA–Houston Chapter
IIA Netherlands
IIA–New York Chapter

Visionary Circle
The Family of Lawrence B. Sawyer

Chairman's Circle
Chevron Corporation
ExxonMobil Corporation
Itau Unibanco Holding S.A.
JCPenney Company, Inc.
Lockheed Martin Corporation
Southern California Edison Company

Diamond Donor
IIA–Central Ohio Chapter
IIA–San Jose Chapter